THE ART OF GETTING BUSINESS ANALYSIS RIGHT

Maria Montgomery
MA, CPC, MCC

First published in 2022 by Maria Montgomery in Melbourne, Australia.

E: mariamontgomery30@gmail.com

Illustrations by Maria Montgomery.

Cover illustration by Maria Montgomery and You Exec presentations template.

Images: chapters 1 and 2 by Dreamstime, chapters 4 to 7 by Maria Montgomery and You Exec presentations template.

To Rob, Eavan and Mia.
Thank you!!! I love you all heaps.

Contents

Foreword

My why?

I wrote this book because I'm passionate about developing people and teams and, most importantly, getting things in life like business analysis done right. So, I've decided to share my business analysis journey, my wealth of experience and my knowledge with you.

My aim is to get you inspired to do business analysis the right way.

Now, let me take you on a journey in my shoes into the world of business analysis.

I'm based in Melbourne, Australia, and live with my husband and two teenage kids, who keep me entertained daily.

Throughout my career, working from junior to leadership/management levels, I have experienced how hard it is to get business analysis done the right way. While moving between different organisations and industries, I have discovered common core ingredients to getting business analysis right. What I was dealing with in one organisation ended up being identical to the issues I'd uncovered in another. I was applying relatively consistent core skills and techniques to similar problems.

My passion for putting ideas on paper, drawing process maps and analysing different concepts, ideas, inputs, outputs and flows (positive and negative flows) saw me progress to various leadership levels and have a successful career in business analysis. Analysis is a great way to unpack and look at things differently and find other pathways and options.

As an expert in business analysis, I ask myself if it is possible to get greater than 50% of analysis right. Business analysis is harder in practice to get right more than 50% of the time!

After reading this book, based on my experience in implementing these types of changes in organisations, I am confident you can achieve at least 50% improvements in your business analysis outcomes. Sound interesting?

This book intends to familiarise readers with key business analysis concepts, terminology, principles and capabilities. It will provide you with guides and tips on doing the best work to get business analysis right in your workplace. It is intended for anyone who wants to understand and apply business analysis to make viable changes in improving your organisation and achieving your goals. If, for example, you are an entrepreneur working in a small business, you could embed business analysis skill sets. You will find great value in research by diving deep into ideas, options, benefits and costs. It could save you a lot of time and money in the future.

Introduction

"Begin with the end in mind" is the second of *The 7 Habits of Highly Effective People* by Dr Stephen R Covey. This habit resonated with me when I decided to write this book.

This book has three parts.

Part 1: About business analysis. This part discusses what business analysis is, and the foundation of business analysis. Until we understand the value of business analysis and its impacts if not done right, it is tough to understand the importance of getting business analysis right.

Part 2: Skills to get business analysis right and build the best team of business analysts (BAs). This part focuses on skills, both individual and team competences, and the importance of having the right model and processes to develop yourself and your team and build a thriving business analysis community and practice. These are components that have helped me build a successful team, capability and culture.

Part 3: Leadership that builds the best BAs and business analysis practice. This part describes how to be successful in the business analysis world, you need to provide strong leadership in building and supporting the best BA team and practice.

The conclusion will outline seven key ingredients, the magic, to get business analysis right, more than 50% of the time.

PART 1
About business analysis

What does business analysis mean?
What do we do in the business analysis world?

You may be just starting a career in business analysis. You may be a senior business analyst and never stop to reflect on what business analysis really is. Even though I've been in this industry for over two decades now, I don't usually stop and think about what business analysis is. I recall applying for a business analyst role with Terra Firma (an IT consulting company) in 2011. As part of the application process, I was asked to sit a test; the test started with the question "Describe what business analysis is." I was surprised at the simplicity of the question. At the time, I had been a business analyst for seven years and it was a question I should have easily been able to answer. The truth is that I needed to think about it.

Part 1 will look at what business analysis is in three sections:

- what is business analysis and its phases (Chapter 1)
- the value of business analysis and the impact of not getting it right (Chapter 2)
- the foundation of analysis (Chapter 3).

Before reading on, please pause for a minute. Ask yourself what business analysis means to you. Write it down on a piece of paper, then reflect on your answer after reading Part 1.

Chapter 1

What is business analysis?

Business analysis is a professional discipline identifying business needs and determining solutions to business problems.

"Business analysis is the practice of enabling change in an enterprise by defining needs and recommending solutions that deliver value to stakeholders. Business analysis enables an enterprise to articulate needs and the rationale for change, and to design and describe solutions that can deliver value."[1]

Business analysis is about using **insights from data** (that you have access to or have captured using appropriate business analysis techniques) to clearly identify business needs and existing pain points. The key to analysis is gathering, finding and investigating detailed information to inform and support possible solutions. Data is essential to business analysis; you need data to support solution options to present to stakeholders, and to assist them in decision-making.

For example, suppose there is a manual process that requires a banker to complete a form and one option is to replace the manual entry with an automated solution. In this example, data on the volume of applications processed and the time taken to complete a form manually is crucial to understanding whether an automated solution is worthwhile; this data will feed into the cost-benefit analysis. The valuable information that the business analysis captures will provide significant input into the business case and decision.

From a personal perspective, I greatly enjoy hearing my mentees tell me what they have learned through my mentorship program. Here is what they said about business analysis:

- It helps you understand problems and see them through a stakeholder lens by not getting bogged down in a solution mode or your own opinion.
- It offers an understanding of stakeholder needs and pain points, ensuring you don't go into solution mode.
- It facilitates and outlines the stakeholders' needs, wants, options and benefits by analysing supportive data.
- You can identify business needs and find solutions to various problems.

1 IIBA (International Institute of Business Analysis), *A Guide to the Business Analysis Body of Knowledge (BABOK® Guide)*, iiba.org, 2015, p 2., accessed 13 February 2023.

- Understand how role of individual in organisations fulfil the organisation's purpose or vision.
- It can help businesses identify problems and issues to work through and come up with solutions to various problems.
- It can synthesise information provided by various members of an organisation.

Now that we have the business analysis covered, what does getting the business analysis right mean to you?

After working on many large transformational projects and in personal settings, I often questioned how analysis could be part of what I do right. Getting business analysis right **is not about being right, it is about getting it right**.

The evolution of business analysis

Let's go back to where it all began. Once upon a time, in the 1940s, business analysis started as a practice when the first programmable computer was birthed. Computer systems were used mainly by the governments, universities and the organisations that invented them.

These organisations could have been more efficient. For example, storing data was complex due to the large amount of space it required. Communication could have been easier among programmers. In this context, the business analyst (BA) role was born.

The importance of the business analyst role has been recognised in the last decade. I remember the day I started my career in the business analysis space (over twenty-eight years ago) as a junior business analyst in 1994 at Ansett Australia (the airline no longer exists). I was quickly tasked with gathering, analysing, validating and documenting various business needs and process maps. I had an aha moment, and quickly realised that the topics covered at my university while studying the Bachelor of Business in Information Technology, such as process maps, were really used in real life situations. While studying, I could not see the value in creating process maps. At the time, the role of business analyst had just started to become known in the IT industry. I decided then that I wanted to build my career as a business analyst.

Growing up, I was always an analyst at heart. I have a passion for finding solutions and understanding how things work. I analysed everything I did back in Serbia, where I spent my childhood. I constantly asked my mother questions about everything, which drove her crazy.

The evolution of the role of the business analyst

Business analysts are passionate about what we do and our role is not shrinking; it is evolving. Initially, the role was referred to as a system analyst. Now in the industry we find three distinct roles exist: business analysts, technical analysts and process analysts. The importance of the business analyst has been recognised in the last decade as more and more companies seek technological solutions to complicated business problems. Business analysts are getting more involved in strategic analysis as well.

Particularly in the last decade, the business analyst's role has changed to keep up with the latest business needs as there are more readily available technological solutions to complicated business problems. For example, business analysts are now getting more involved in strategic analysis and planning at the start of a project's initiation or concept phase.

The analysis is a process

"Computers are useless. They can only answer."
—Pablo Picasso[2]

Analysis is a process. It brings structure to the method of understanding, planning and articulating needs; it is a process and technique for understanding and identifying business needs, validating them and finding solutions to various business-related problems.

In summary, a process for analysing is to identify the following:

- business needs and problems that need to be resolved
- strategies for identifying better ways of working and key stakeholders, and evaluating possible solutions
- applying good decision-making mechanisms
- well-established estimations to ensure you have the right project coverage and team to soldier on and get the work done.

There are several phases of a project or initiative that business analysts undertake as part of the process:

- discovery (aka scoping)
- initiation and planning
- execution (build, test, release)
- monitoring and control.

Project closure should also be mentioned here, seeing that business analyst involvement is usually required.

2 C Priest, 'Computers Are Useless; They Only Give You Answers', DataRobot blog, 29 September 2017, accessed 14 February 2023.

The most important phase to me is the discovery phase, also known as the scoping phase, where key needs are discovered. In this phase, pain points and solution options are elaborated on and assessed, and requirements are elicited (and validated with the key stakeholders). Business analysts are key players and have direct influence on the overall success of the project.

Discovery phase

The discovery phase is **the stage where information is collected and analysed**, and the project's intended market, audience and stakeholders are identified. It involves articulating a well-defined and in-depth understanding of the goals, scope and limitations of the project.

The discovery phase is the initial phase, where you conduct investigations before a specific initiative or project has been kicked off. You can clearly understand a need; you focus on identifying goals you are trying to achieve and problems that need to be solved, ensuring it is beneficial to continue with the initiative.

During this phase, as a business analyst, you will facilitate testing the idea and problem you are trying to resolve, ensuring the business needs and expectations are met. The stakeholders and sponsors will know what they want or the product they desire.

You may not necessarily be clear on their goals or expectations of what needs to be delivered as a final product. This may lead to a mismatch in your stakeholders' and sponsor's expectations.

It is critical to ask the following questions:

- What are the problems the business is trying to solve?
- What are the key objectives and goals they are trying to reach?
- Why do they have this problem?
- How might they solve this problem?

Initiation and planning phase

During the initiation phase, you will be required to work closely with your key stakeholders and produce or update the high-level process maps and business requirements (also known as stakeholder requirements). At this stage of the project, the business case should also be approved. As a leader or a senior business analyst you will be required to provide a business analysis plan (this is covered further in the Skills and techniques section of this book).

Execution (design, build) phase

Once the initiation phase has been completed, you will need to work closer with your key stakeholders to produce lower-level process maps (for example, levels 3, 4) and further elaborate on the business requirements to a detailed level (functional requirements), document business and functional requirements, and prepare a requirements traceability matrix (RTM), also covered further in the Skills and techniques section in this book. Additionally, business analysts need to assist with risk management activity by raising change requests, issues and risks, as required.

Monitoring and control, closure phase

In this final phase of the project, business analysts generally support management and validation of complete and approved requirements.

KEY TAKEAWAYS

- Business analysis is about using insights from data to identify business needs and pain points. When analysing information, it is essential to further break the data into things that need to:
    - change
    - stay the same
    - be included
    - are missing.
- Business analysis is important because it provides organisations with the tools and processes needed to make informed decisions, better manage resources and achieve improved outcomes. It is essential for helping organisations define their objectives and strategies, analyse markets and competitors, and establish processes for contin-

ual improvement. The analysis also helps organisations align its operations and processes with its business objectives. Furthermore, it can help organisations identify and understand their strengths, weaknesses, opportunities and threats (SWOT), and create plans for achieving their desired outcomes.
- Once the business needs and pain points are identified, then recommendations for changes that provide value to the stakeholder/s are made.
- You must ensure the business needs and expectations are met, by facilitating the testing of ideas and problems you are trying to resolve.
- It is critical to ask the right questions to understand and clearly articulate stakeholders' and sponsors' business needs.

ACTION YOU CAN TAKE

Make sure you have a clear understanding of what business analysis is and its process. While you may require training in some areas, ultimately, it's the little things that you can do like self-guided study.

Take time to learn the best ways to capture the business's needs and expectations, and ask the right questions. I used to set aside time every Friday from 5:00pm to 5:30pm to assess my week, and put actions against gaps in my knowledge areas and business analysis tasks. I also looked at things that I could have done better. At one stage, my key focus was on finding better ways of capturing key business needs and pain points for difficult stakeholders. My action was to find YouTube videos, podcasts or internal company training. I would then schedule in my calendar to undertaking this self-guided training. I enjoyed YouTube and podcasts as I was able to listen and learn while exercising early in the morning every work day between 6:30am and 7:30am.

By reading books, listening to podcasts and learning from peers, you can obtain valuable knowledge.

Chapter 2

Value of business analysis and impacts of not getting it right

"One of the key reasons we need to get requirements right is that requirements errors account for 70% to 85% of project rework."
—Leffingwell, 1997[3]

3 D Leffingwell, '*Managing Software Requirements*', Addison Wesley Publisher, 1999.

Getting business analysis **right** is imperative to being successful in any project or initiative. Recently, I have noticed a great demand for business analysts, and business analysts' jobs are advertised across many different industries, such as health, aged care and transport. The business analysis skill set is valuable and needed. Yet, business analysts are in significant shortage. For all these reasons you may want to consider a career as a business analyst.

Business analysts are at the forefront of the strategic and conceptual project phase since we can speak not only to technological solutions but also about how they can be implemented to meet market desires. This is how businesses achieve a competitive advantage, not by wasting time and resources on re-writes, maintenance and defects, but by putting action in motion to use technology to better reach out to and solve problems for customers. The business analyst plays a key role in making that vision a reality.

I still find organisations trying to discover the value of business analysts because the role is changing faster now than ever. I have worked on many transformational projects and experienced the role of the business analyst consistently evolving from business, process and technical analysis perspectives.

Current challenges and problems

Many painful challenges and problems can be experienced during a project, resulting in an inability to achieve the desired outcome. Here are some of the key challenges I experience in my work:

- *Lack of a centralised business analysis community.* This results in inconsistent business analysis approaches and outputs. Organisations and projects follow different methodologies and use different tools to deliver business analysis services.
- *Lack of clarity of business analysts' roles and responsibilities.* Business analysts' roles and responsibilities may not be clearly defined in constantly changing environments. For example, I've seen uncertainty

introduced when the delivery methodology changes from Waterfall to Agile.

- *Stakeholders' expectations.* Stakeholders often have inconsistent beliefs about the role of business analysts: our responsibilities, who we should interact with, and what we should deliver. This can create friction when dealing with some stakeholders.
- *Constant re-planning, scope crep or even lack of planning on projects.* Business analysts are faced with unrealistic expectations when there is a lack of planning or re-planning. Business analysts must be able to work with this and start and deliver quickly to meet a specific deadline.
- *Constant upskilling.* Business analysts need to constantly upskill to remain relevant and become better at our trade. Technology is constantly changing (e.g., cloud-based solutions, microservices, etc.) and, while business analysts don't need to have a deep understanding of these technologies, we need to have a competent level of understanding to allow us to understand the constraints faced by implementation teams in delivering business requirements.

Some projects will require knowledge in a specific domain (e.g., superannuation, insurance, defence, health, retail, etc.). Working in finance, I've discovered the importance of specific product knowledge (e.g., options pricing). Again, the business analyst does not need to be a subject matter expert, but we need to gain enough knowledge to understand what the business does and wants, and to be able to convey this to the delivery teams.

- *Retaining competent business analysts.* The current business analysis resource market is hot. We are in demand. I often get requests from project managers to secure quality business analysts only to find that I cannot easily source them in the current climate.

Understanding these challenges is essential. You will need to overcome them to get business analysis done right. Ignoring these challenges can have a severe impact on a project; it can lead to poor outcomes and cost overruns.

Impacts of poor business analysis

Let's look at the 'why'. Why is business analysis so important?

"The major consequence of requirements problems is rework – doing over something you thought was already done – late in development or after release. Few software organizations measure how much of their development effort they expend on rework; those who do often get scary numbers. Studies have shown that rework can consume 40 to 50 percent of your total development costs (Charette 2005). Requirements errors alone account for 70 to 85 percent of the rework cost (Leffingwell 1997)."[4]

Now you might be thinking, what does it take to capture good requirements? In his article, Karl Wiegers explains that, "The major consequence of requirements problem(s) is rework."

No one likes rework. It is **annoying** and it is **costly**.

KEY TAKEAWAYS

- From experience, I've seen the following impacts of not getting business requirements right:
  - Delayed project delivery. Without proper requirements, it can be difficult to estimate project timelines and lead times, resulting in projects taking longer to complete than expected.
  - Cost overruns. This is especially true if development and testing efforts need to be extended due to the lack of clear requirements or if features need to be revised and built out to meet the needs of stakeholders.
- It is effective when BAs are at the head of the concept or discovery phases of projects since they can speak about technology and how it should be implemented to meet the market's desires.
- It is important to get requirements right, as errors will increase time required to be spent on rework and overall project's cost.

4 K Wiegers, When Bad Requirements Happen To Good People, medium.com, 23 October 2023, accessed 13 February 2023.

ACTION YOU CAN TAKE

Impacts of not getting business analysis right have a big impact on the success of every project. You need to understand the impact and ensure you take every step in getting the business requirements done right. I encourage you to do the following:

1. Write down on Post-it notes three impacts you have experienced or learnt in this book on not getting business requirements right. (5 minutes)
2. Create short sentences (4 to 8 words) against each impact on what you can do to mitigate the impact. (10 minutes)
3. Review each sentence and see if there is anything else you would like to add. (10 minutes)
4. Put your Post-it notes on your laptop or working area where you can see them. Reflect on these when you are eliciting requirements and planning your business analysis activities.

Chapter 3

Foundation of analysis

A solid foundation is key to successful business analysis.

The foundation of a business analysis is essential.

Most things you do need some form of foundation. A solid foundation is key to being successful. A solid foundation keeps you grounded as you take small steps to success.

In the context of analysis, basic foundations will provide the underlying basis for business analysis and assist you to ultimately work towards your goal of getting it right. Business analysis is, after all, a professional discipline to identify business needs and facilitate the determination of solutions to business problems.

It is like building a new house – every house needs a strong foundation.

Figure 3.1 identifies current state of the house, why there is a need to develop and the future state new modern house.

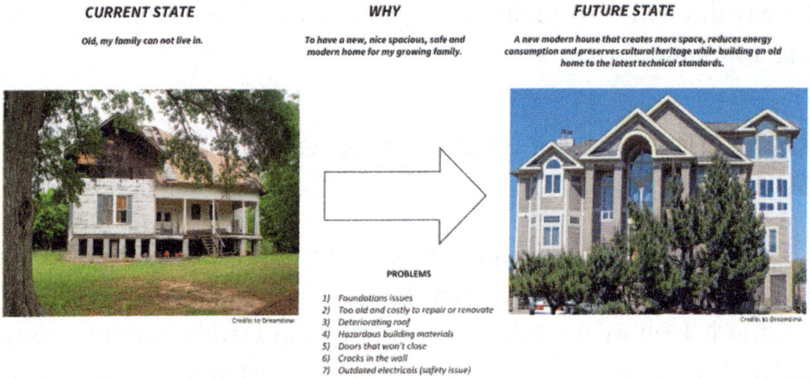

Figure 3.1. Building a new house project

Let's look at the scenario of building a house or unit, in Figure 3.1. The right foundation is important to keep your home safe. So, how do you define what must be included in the foundation of a house? You need to start by looking at the bigger picture: what would you like your house to look like? What do you want to build? Are you planning to have a place with ten bedrooms, a swimming pool, a tennis court, an underground cellar? These could be seen as our high-level needs and wants (in this case, personal or family needs).

Ask these questions to establish foundations:

- Is it needed?
- Who needs it?
- Why do they need it?
- What is the end goal they are trying to achieve?
- What are the things they must have to achieve their goals (for example, features you can't live without)?

A need represents a requirement to solve a problem or achieve a specific objective. It is important to prioritise requirements as prioritisation provides transparency and allows decisions to be made when contemplating what to include in the scope of any project you may conduct. There is almost always limited budget, and you must target to maximise value and minimise costs (where possible).

Some techniques to get business analysis foundations right

It is important to distinguish between must-have and nice-to-have features, as an example from my own life will demonstrate. I recently built a new house. I felt we *needed* three bedrooms and a study to accommodate our family members. My husband told me that he felt we *needed* concrete heating. I said no to the concrete heating due to the extra cost; it was not a must-have feature for me. After some discussion, we agreed that concrete heating was a nice-to-have feature of the house and decided not to include this in the build. Once our must-have needs were agreed upon, we went ahead and built a house to meet all these must-have needs and decided to forgo the nice-to-have needs to reduce costs.

If you don't identify your must-have and nice-to-have needs, you may end up with incorrect requirements and undesirable products. In my case, I misdiagnosed the concrete heating as a nice-to-have and we ended up with a house that takes a while to warm up and can be cold in some areas. I have been trying to fix this problem by adding electrical heaters, which ended up costing more. And of course, we can't change it now as it is too late; the foundations and concreting have already been completed. To me, this was a nice-to-have feature; on the other hand, to my husband, it was a must-have, and to reduce costs he compromised his must-have needs. In this case I incorrectly prioritised my requirements.

You might be able to relate this to projects you have worked on. How often do you have to focus on the costs and budgets allocated to a project, and the requirements are comprised and may end up reprioritised? You may end up implementing various workarounds due to budget constraints or the reprioritisation of requirements, and your client or stakeholder may not end up with the exact product they were looking for in the first place. It is essential to question and focus on the quality of collaboration when identifying and prioritising needs. In my case, I do wish that I had collaborated with my husband better and seen his point of view. Ouch!! Did I say that? 😊

And how does this relate to getting the analysis right? It is not just in our professional and in our everyday lives; we are faced with looking at our needs and using our analytical mindset to get them right. For example, in a house situation, I had to think of the questions such as:

- **Drivers:** Why do we need a new house? (Our previous house was old, too small and required too much maintenance.)
- **Stakeholders:** *Who* needs it? (Two adults, two kids.)
- **Requirements:** *What* are the features of the house we need and want? (We needed three bedrooms.)
- **Timeline:** *When* do we need it done? (Yesterday!!) How long are we prepared to wait for it?
- **Budget:** What is our *budget*?
- **Constraints:** Given your budget, what features are you prepared to *compromise* on?
- **Delivery:** *How* are we going to build it?

The key question that will drive the project, is 'why?' Ensure there is always a quality check or quality control applied to your drivers and requirements. Ask a friend, colleague or someone external to validate and quality check your requirements. Do you know what industry best practices of writing requirements and creating process maps are? Check how you could leverage or use the industry best practices (if appropriate).

Others may have gone through the same journey; you might be able to leverage learnings from them. Be on top of the game and consider as many options as possible.

3 essential techniques to set the foundations for successful business analysis

In the context of business analysis, three key techniques that you need to be clear on for establishing the foundations are:

1. use process maps to understand current state
2. problem-solving
3. future target state.

Current state

What do you understand about the flow of critical activities and the people involved in carrying out each step in a process? Usually, it's helpful to visually describe the sequence of steps performed by actors; this can be done using what's known as 'process maps'. Current state process maps depict what's currently being done in an organisation. I'm a big fan of process maps as a tool to capture current state. They provide a visual representation of who is currently doing what, and in what order, and they leave less room for misinterpretation of the current state.

You will need to ask what the reality is of current processes when commencing a project. Figure 3.2 is an example of establishing the current state process steps for the house example (note this map is at a high level).

While establishing the current state, you will uncover pain points and hot topics experienced as part of the current process, for example, there may be too many manual workarounds.

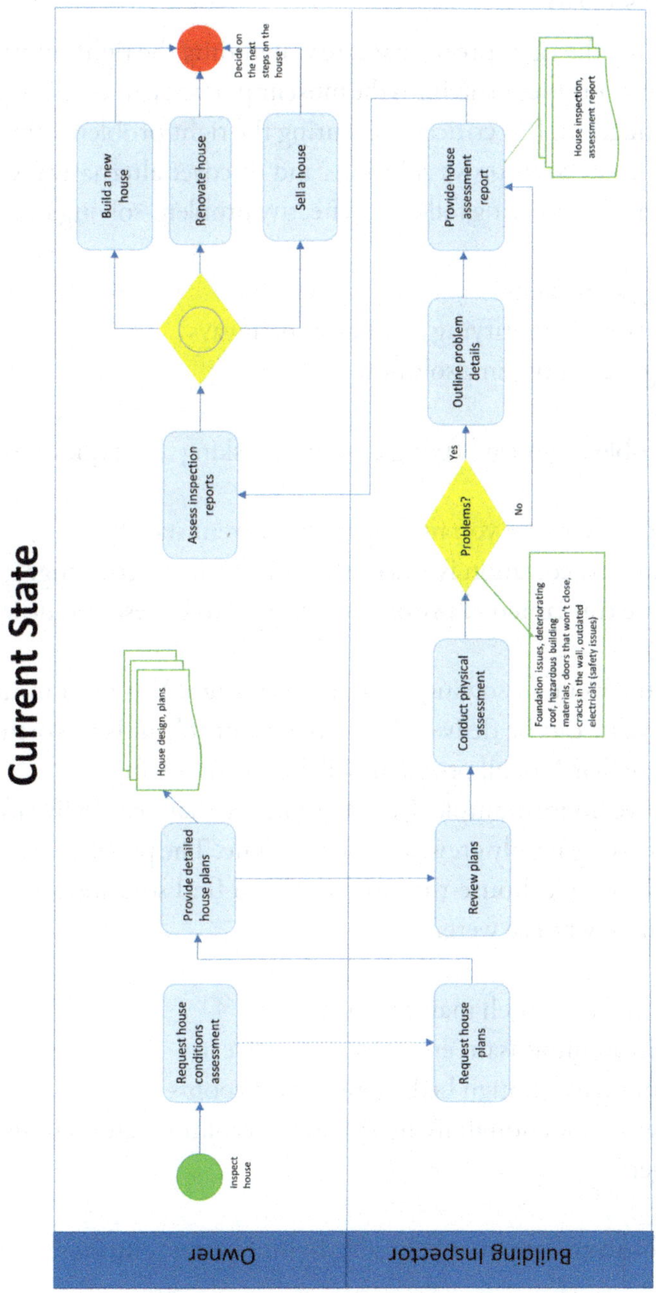

Figure 3.2. Current state house process map

Problem-solving

Are you solving the right problems? Are you finding the right solution to your problems? Problem-solving is the most important part of the business analysis foundation. It is critical in ensuring the right problems are being solved. The key is to improve solutions and discover alternative ways to solve problems, by applying following effective problem-solving strategies:

- defining a problem
- discovery and identifying alternative pathways
- making a decision on a solution.

Define problems you are trying to solve by asking these questions:

- What problems are you finding in the current state?
- What are the common issues or themes you are uncovering?
- What are fundamental problems that need to be resolved now?

Identify the value in solving each of these issues. You need to understand what value can be delivered by solving a problem. Is it worth solving (cost/benefit)? Not all problems will be worth solving.

In the above house example, I wanted a house that I could live in, that was spacious as my family grew, and that was safe. The problems we experienced with our old house that we needed to find solutions for when building our new house were:

- it required too much maintenance
- it was in an unpleasant environment to live in
- it did not have enough bedrooms or bathrooms
- there were not enough living spaces to accommodate a family with teenagers.

As a problem-solver you will be able to find better solutions!

Future target state

We must drill down, understand and ask questions about the future state to assist us to best establish the foundations of a project. Focus on the desirable goals, objectives and benefits you and your client are trying to achieve. Some of the key questions you need to ask are:

- What is the organisation's target state?
- How does this vision add value to the organisation?
- Where will the money be saved or revenue be increased by this target state?
- Which (if any) manual steps do we want to remove and what does the future state look like without these manual processes?
- What is so important about what you are trying to achieve?

It is important for projects to consider wider organisational long-term goals, as the solution may need to be aligned to these goals (for example, an organisation-wide goal is to reduce the cost of sending SMS notifications. The project may need to consider not sending or limiting the number of SMS notifications sent.)

In Figure 3.1 above, a beautiful newly renovated home that reduces energy consumption and preserves cultural heritage with the latest technology standards represents the vision of the future house I wanted to have.

Figure 3.3, below, is an example of the future state process steps for building a new modern dream house, described in the current state. The starting point for this practical map is the house building assessment, as it is the process for future improvements and the house building assessment is a first step.

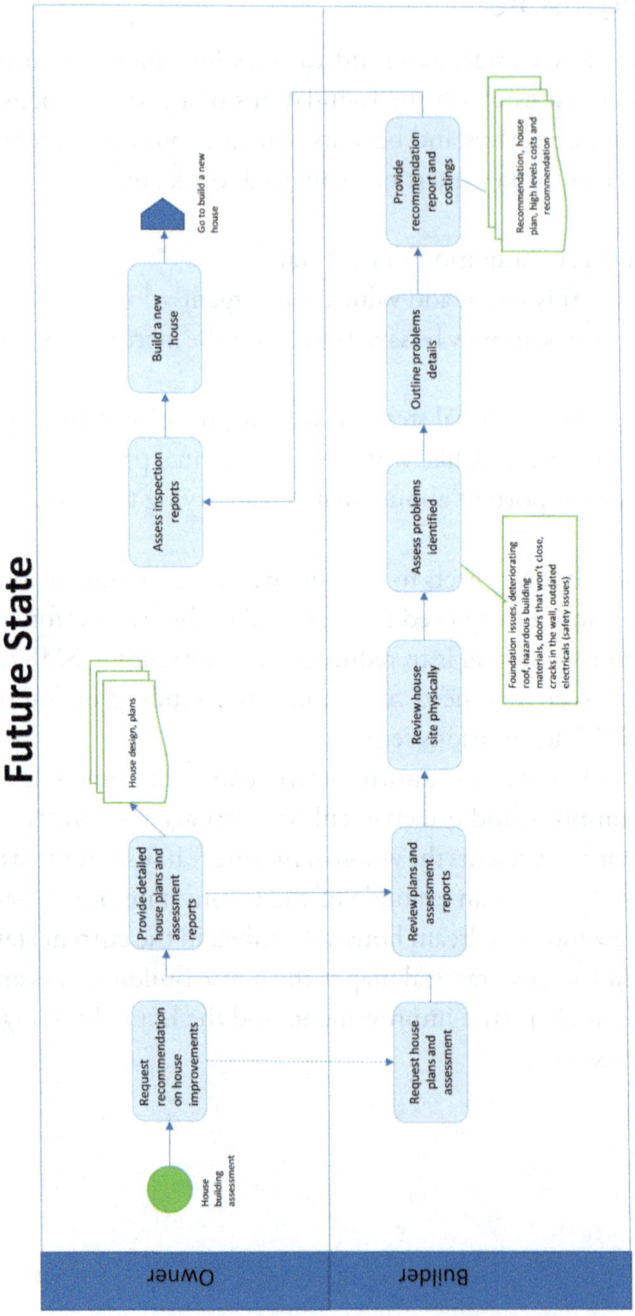

Figure 3.3. Future state: a new modern house process map

Remember, you may not be able to solve all problems at once. In fact, it may not even be sensible to solve *all* the problems you identify – a small problem may be expensive to fix and so, using a cost/benefit assessment, we are better off *not* fixing this problem. Just like getting business analysis right, it is important to ask the right questions to solve the most valuable problems. Though my own experience, I concluded that trying to solve *all* problems is a fool's errand. By reading Oussama Zaskild Malloud's book *How to solve 50% of your problems?*, I settled on the 50% figure when it comes to deciding on which problems to solve.

> *"Everyone has problems in their lives. For the most part, we can quickly solve them without much trouble. We either decide on a quick solution or use a strategy that worked in the past."*
> *— Oussama Zaskild Malloud*[5]

KEY TAKEAWAYS

- It is important to have the foundations of business analysis right because it will provide the underlying basis for business analysis and ensure you get business analysis right. The three essential steps you need be clear on are:
    - use process maps to understand current state
    - problem-solving
    - target state.
- In terms of ensuring the right problems are being solved for in the future target state, ask the following questions:
    1. How can this help you solve the problems or, more importantly, ask yourself what problems are you trying to solve?
    2. What is the most crucial issue you are trying to resolve?
    3. Why is that the most critical problem?

5 OZ Malloud, How to solve 50% of your problems?, 2020.

ACTION YOU CAN TAKE

Reflect on what you wrote down at the beginning of Part 1 about what you think business analysis is and what you can add to that through what you have read in this section.

It is time to start reflecting on what you have learnt so far, using Activity 3.1.

Activity 3.1. Knowledge audit template

Review what you have written down and then reflect on what you have learnt so far. In the table below, write down any gaps or areas you would like to strengthen, and what you will do and when to develop in these areas.

Some examples for knowledge areas, your *what*, tasks and when might include:

- Knowledge area: problem-solving.
- What: I need to straighten my problem-solving skills so that I can assist my stakeholders in identifying better solutions to the problems?
- Tasks: I will do the following tasks. Find self-guided learning I can do by reading books, listening to podcasts and other types of training. Find activities I can do to improve my problem-solving skills. Seek feedback on the project I am working on from my peers.
- When: I will do this by end of this financial year.

Knowledge area	What	Tasks	When

PART 2

Skills to get business analysis right and build the best BA team

Now that you have reflected on the foundation, value and impacts of getting business analysis right, the next step is to learn how to obtain the right skills to build the best business analysis team.

Chapter 4 look at the Getting Business Analysis Right Model, which includes the categories:

1. Governance
2. Design
3. Quality
4. People
5. Relationships
6. Competency.

Chapter 5 covers the competency audit tree, understanding key business analysis knowledge areas and auditing your or your team's skills. These include:

- business analysis planning and monitoring
- elicitation and collaboration
- requirements lifecycle management
- strategy analysis
- Requirements Analysis and Design Definition (RADD)
- solution evaluation.

Chapter 4

The getting business analysis right model

You can get business analysis right.
You may need to be creative, but it is possible.

You may ask, how can I get business analysis right?

With more than twenty years now of being in the analytical world, the following is the business analysis model that has been most effective for me when it comes to getting business analysis right.

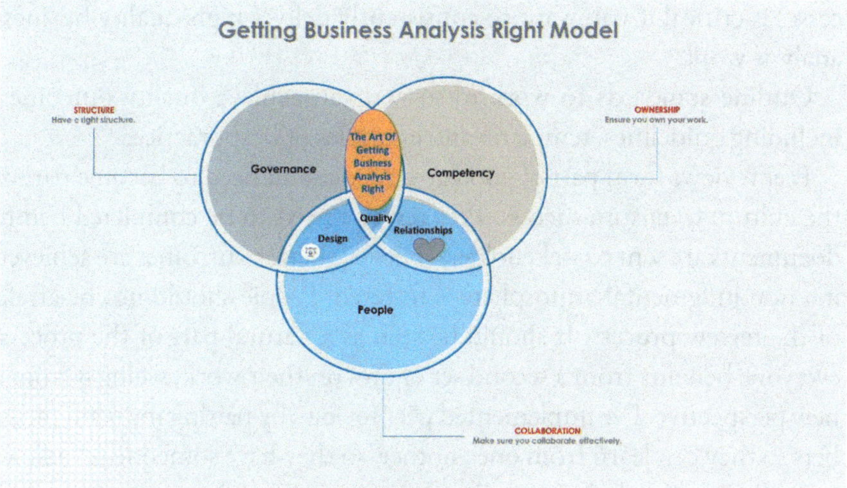

Figure 4.1. Getting Business Analysis Right Model

To get business analysis right and build the best business analysis team, you need to have these categories nailed down:

1. Governance
2. Design
3. Quality
4. People
5. Relationships
6. Competency.

These categories also apply to individuals striving to be the best business analyst in a team or an organisation. Incorporating them into the way that you work will strengthen your professional relationships, capacity and reputation.

Governance

Governance incorporates all the practices and processes that will assist you and your organisation to move in the right direction and stay there. Exceptional governance and embedding appropriate governance processes is critical if you want to consistently deliver high-quality business analysis work.

Outline standards to work to so you can achieve quality outcomes, including guidelines, templates and examples of best practice.

Peer reviews form part of good governance and need to become part of the culture to ensure success. Peer reviews need to be completed before documents are sent to stakeholders. I believe better outcomes are achieved if a non-judgmental atmosphere is fostered. People should not be afraid of the review process. It should be seen as a natural part of the process; everyone benefits from a second set of eyes on their work, seeing it from a new perspective. I've implemented peer reviews by pairing my team members so they can learn from one another, so they have someone to lean on and someone to ask them tough questions to get the best outcomes.

Having a well-prepared stakeholder matrix is also important. A stakeholder matrix must include your sponsor, team members and impacted teams. This is to ensure that the right people are consulted to capture and approve requirements.

Work as a team in this area. Help each other out. I have learnt from reading Karl Wiegers work that to improve the quality of software you need to embed a formal review to investigate most critical or 'open to errors' areas.

"My general rule is: Review early and often, formally and informally."
— Karl Wiegers[6]

Additionally, it is imperative to ensure your work is compliant with any regulatory bodies (based on the industry you might be working in,

6 K Wiegers, Requirements Review Challenges, medium.com, 10 February 2020, accessed 13 February 2023.

such as the Australian Prudential Regulation Authority, or APRA, if you are working with a financial organisation), as well as the business analysis industry standards, such as the International Institute of Business Analysis (IIBA).

IIBA sets the standard for business analysis, the ***global standard***. IIBA is dedicated to establishing and maintaining the highest standards, regulations and best practice for both business analysis practices and individual business analysts. Make sure you jump on board with IIBA, check out the suggested standards, join the group and be part of the tribe. IIBA provides tremendous support in the IIBA space, including forums and webinars. It's an invaluable resource and well worth tapping into.

Structure

It is important to have the right structure for your team and organisation, including:

- practices
- standards (such as alignment to the IIBA)
- tools.

These are further elaborated on in the Skills and techniques section in this book.

I recommend having a business analysis framework, which is useful for any organisation or project to provide conceptual structure and guidance. You may consider producing a BA framework to clearly articulate all crucial requirements for getting the business done. The purpose of a BA framework is to:

- provide guidance on eliciting requirements and identifying business outcomes
- identify when fit for purpose business requirements and processes are needed
- ensure appropriate quality control.

Design

The very nature of a business analyst is analytical and this is unlikely to change, especially in an era of rapid digital transformation. However, this doesn't mean that certain concepts of design thinking can't be applied in practice to the role of a business analyst. Design thinking is in essence just another form of business analysis, and many business analysts will have used design thinking concepts in projects before.

Perhaps the most common areas that business analysts can apply design thinking to are scope definition, requirements elicitation and analysis, and decision validation. The depth and length of the process will largely depend on the scale and complexity of individual projects, and as organisations are becoming increasingly agile so too will the concepts that business analysts are required to use.

Quality

You need to **design high-quality** performance into every aspect of your business analysis work, including, but not limited to:

- templates or examples of quality outputs
- mentoring
- reviews
- approval processes.

Design your standards with guidelines, frameworks and templates examples, and share them with your team. Make sure you have samples of what good quality requirements look like, and what bad requirements look like.

Scope management is another important step that you need to have a process for. During my career, I have experienced many projects with scope creep.

People

A vital part of a business analyst's role is working closely with people, including our own team members. Working well with people can contribute enormously to the successful delivery of business analysis outcomes.

Collaboration

Make sure you collaborate effectively. Effective collaboration is key to successful requirements gathering and to the success of any project. The secret to effective collaboration is to:

- ensure the **right** people are involved
- have a well-prepared stakeholder matrix, and ensure that everyone knows what they are accountable for
- have a clear understanding of analysis purpose and needs
- tune into your impacted stakeholders and systems
- set the **right business analysis** expectations which will provide:
    - clarity for your stakeholders and project team members
    - get everyone on the same page
    - enhance communication
    - help prevent confusion.

Collaboration makes a more efficient team. Set the expectations at the start of a project or piece of work you are assigned to. It improves the way your team works together and solves problems.

My favourite saying is from Stephen Covey: "Seek first to understand, then to be understood."[7]

Collaboration is essential in everything you do to understand your purpose and needs as a business analyst. Ensure you are flexible. Collaborative adaption is about being flexible – it supports teamwork, improves creativity and enhances overall value to the business. Change is happening, and teams must be prepared.

7 S Covey, 'The 7 Habits of Highly Effective People', Simon & Schuster Australia Publisher, 1 June 2020.

Teams and organisations have to change quickly; if your team isn't aligned, it's easy for change to lead to disaster.

If you are dealing with vendors, you will have multiple external stakeholders. How do you work with them? We can't control our vendors' quality, or can we? You need to establish and agree on a set of acceptable standards initially with your vendor, during the planning phase. Provide them with a sample, templates and guidelines on the required deliverables, and introduce a governance and quality check process where you or your team members review and provide feedback to the vendor.

Projects are set for disaster if teams do not work together, collaborate and build healthy relationships across projects!

Relationships

At the heart of business analysis is people and creating trusting relationships with them.

This is the emotional starting point for building trustful, healthy relationships. It is important for you and your team members to communicate with each other in a safe, trusting and transparent manner. Make sure your team members are engaged. Encourage open communication and participation. It's essential that as a team you can share ideas, add new processes and tools where required, and that the right people are involved.

I have encountered similarly challenging stakeholders when moving between different organisations. Within the financial sector, I kept coming across the 'accountant-type' of stakeholder. I recognise them quickly; they don't like to be told what to do and they don't like to be quizzed too much.

I tailor my approach when collaborating with them. I think about what information I need from them and how I can get it. I end up drawing lots of T-account ledgers (a graphic representation of a general ledger that records business transactions such as debit and credit) to understand their needs, to see things from their perspective. This change in approach works well. I can then create trusting relationships with my key stakeholders. As they say, it became 'happy days'.

Make sure you have a close and healthy relationship with:

- program and project managers
- stakeholders, such as project sponsors, product owners, subject matter experts (SMEs) and process owners
- project team members such as change managers, change analysts, communications specialists and process analysts
- enterprise, business and solution architects.

Engage with them on a personal level. Take them out for a coffee or lunch. Learn what they like and what they don't like. Understand their point of view and what they need from you.

Competency

To get consistently good outcomes, you need people who know what they are doing. People with high levels of competency. So, you need to invest in people's skills and capacity. It is essential to balance business analysis competency levels in business analysis practice by upskilling.

"The right person for the right project has now been selected and everyone can get to work. To keep the BA engaged in the project, implement a plan to manage and support them throughout the project."
—Jeff Martin[8]

Make sure you spend valuable time understanding the **professional development** that you and your team need. To be successful you need many skills and competencies. I strongly recommend looking for a mentor or coach to learn a new skill from or to guide you toward your team's career development goals. For example, you or your team member's goal might be to be a senior business analyst in two years. I have personally coached many individuals in achieving their personal and professional goals. I have guided them through the lens of my experience.

8 J Martin, 'The Right Business Analyst, the Right Project', modern analyst.com, accessed 13 February 2023.

Investing time in training and getting specific certifications in your field is also just as important. Even though I've been in the Agile environment for an extended period, I made sure to obtain IIBA Agile analysis certifications, and now run study groups. You should never stop learning! I still see business analysts being expected to know everything. I can closely relate to the saying, "We are jacks of all trades and master of none!"

It also pays off to **ensure the right people are involved**. When undertaking analysis within your organisation, project or initiative, it is imperative to ensure the right people are involved at the appropriate stages of your project or initiative. As described in the next point, complete a well-defined stakeholder matrix to meet this objective.

Ownership

Ownership in competency is an important skill to have and it is used as an instrument to create value. You need to know what to own, how to own it and when to own it?

Don't wait for your leader, manager, project manager or key stakeholder to follow up on your deliverables. Ask your teammates for help if you need to if you don't understand your stakeholder. When completing deliverables, make sure you revalidate them, ask someone to review them. If, for example, it is a senior stakeholder you might be dealing with, make sure you provide a summary of what you are asking them to review and add additional documentation so that they can review them. I have found the faster way to get a need or a message across is through outlining key points and provided necessary analysis data to support it.

KEY TAKEAWAYS

- Make sure you have all categories covered: governance (including structure), design, quality, people (including collaboration), relationships and competency (including ownership).
- You need to take ownership of the project, take pride in your work, and always add value. You take ownership by believing that taking action is not someone else's responsibility.

- Ensure you take initiative in asking appropriate questions, making sure that quality work is produced.
- Ensure that you are familiar with the industry standards, such as the International Institute of Business Analysis (IIBA). IIBA provides a wealth of knowledge and access to valuable reading material.

ACTION YOU CAN TAKE

You must allocate time to self-validate your knowledge in all categories covered in the Getting Business Analysis Right Model. The list of what it takes to do well below is based on what I have come across time after time when working as a business analyst.

Activity 4.1. So, what does it take to do well checklist

Tick those that you need to learn and find out more about.

People

☐ Communicate continuously and consistently by creating trusting relationships with your stakeholders, project and team members.

Structure

☐ Have the right structure for your team and organisation (practices, standards, service catalogues, tools).

Ownership

☐ Take ownership of the project, take pride in your work and add value.

Collaboration

☐ Ensure the right people are involved.

☐ Have a well-prepared stakeholder matrix.

☐ Have a clear understanding of analysis purpose and needs.

- ☐ Tune into your impacted stakeholders and systems.
- ☐ Set the right business analysis expectations.

Governance

- ☐ Ensure good governance.
- ☐ Design high-quality performance (scope, strong requirements standards, quality, etc.)
- ☐ Conduct detailed groundwork to capture requirements by working with a change team to identify potential impacts.

Competency

- ☐ Having the right balance of the BA competency levels in the BA practice or organisation by upskilling and learning.
- ☐ Conduct BA professional development (mentoring, coaching and training).
- ☐ Regularly undertake your competency skills audit.

Pause and think about the categories you most need help with to understand more about what it takes to get business analysis right.

Chapter 5

Competency audit tree

The business analysis world is complex.

The business analysis world is complex. The following tree shows just how complex and extensive business analysis competency is. The tree highlights some of the most common knowledge areas and skills I've used in the past. But it is not a comprehensive list; there are more. I've aligned (where appropriate) the business analyst competencies to the IIBA standard – the *Guide to Business Analysis Body of Knowledge* version 3.0 (BABOK® Guide). Although the BABOK® Guide outlines five key knowledge areas, I have grouped the concepts as follows:

1. business analysis planning and monitoring
2. strategy analysis
3. elicitation and collaboration
4. requirements management encompasses requirements deliverables and requirements lifecycle management
5. skills and techniques encompass skills essential by BAs and techniques BAs need to be competent.

The big green leaves in the diagram that follows represent core business analysis knowledge areas and skills (must haves), with an underlining subset of small green leaves highlighting skills (skills, behaviours, characteristics and knowledge areas that support core competencies). The grey shapes display techniques, tools and tasks used to support the successful delivery of each knowledge area.

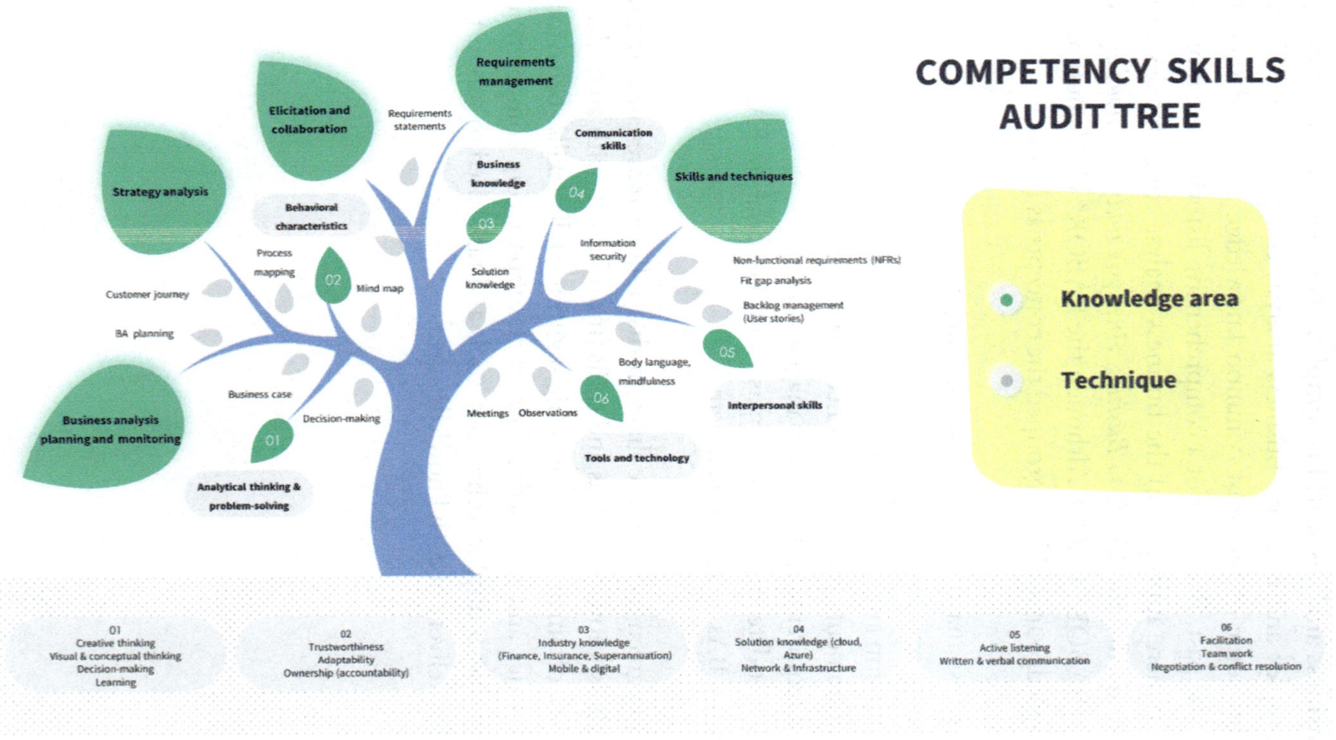

Figure 5.1. Competency audit tree

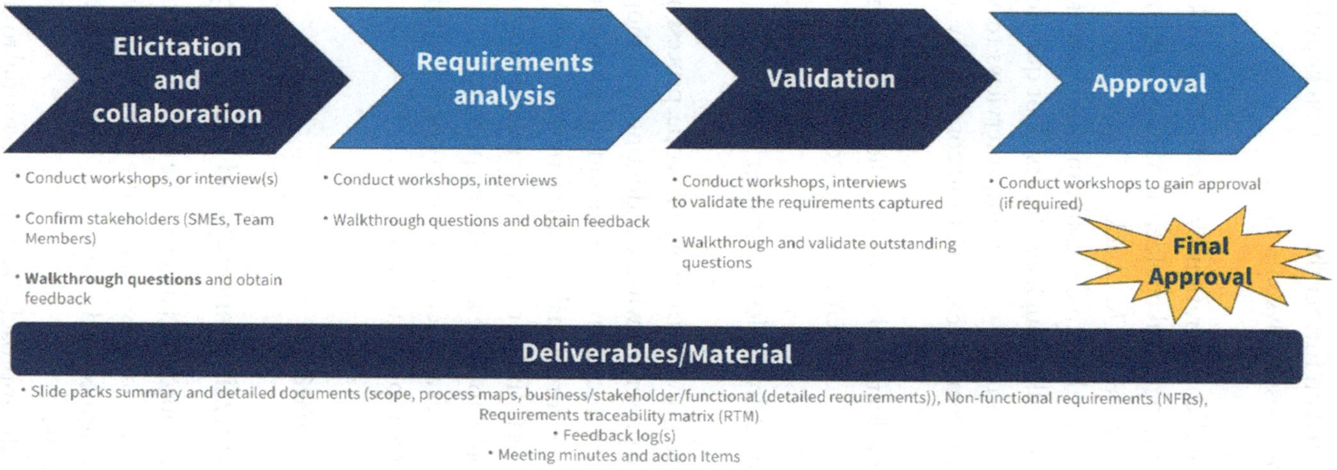

Figure 5.2. Activities performed at various steps in business analysis

These are elaborated on further the next section knowledge areas.

Key steps in business analysis include:

- elicitation and collaboration by conducting workshops and interviews with the right stakeholders (SMEs or team members) to walk through questions and feedback
- requirements analysis to deep dive into analysis of the information obtained and walkthrough any feedback or questions.
- validation to conduct workshops, interviews to validate information and requirements captured and confirm any outstanding questions
- approval conduct workshops or follow up via email to gain final approval on the requirements captured.

The materials and deliverables to consider include:

- slide packs to provide summary on scope, process maps and requirements to be presented when conducting workshops or interviews
- requirements documentation including process maps, business / stakeholder / functional (detailed requirements), non-functional requirements (NFRs), requirements traceability matrix (RTM)
- feedback log(s) to track all feedback provided
- meeting minutes and action items to document what was discussed in each workshop or interview.

Knowledge areas

1. Business analysis planning and monitoring

Business analysis approaches describe the overall method followed when performing business analysis work on any given initiative, how and when tasks will be performed and monitoring of how BA work and deliverables were delivered.

Regardless of the approach, planning is essential to ensure that value is delivered to an enterprise. Planning occurs more than once each initiative as plans are updated to address changing business conditions. Monitoring encompasses the assessment of how BA work was completed to ensure expectations were met, and areas for future improvements are understood.

2. Strategy analysis

The business analyst's role in strategic analysis is to identify the internal or external strengths and weaknesses that directly impact organisational growth. The Strength, Weakness, Opportunity, Threat (SWOT) analysis is a great technique to identify an organisation's strength and weaknesses. A SWOT analysis can assist with assessing possible solutions to a problem, making decisions on the most appropriate path to undertake on an initiative. For example, an initiative or project might propose the introduction of a new digital tool, which may allow an organisation to reach a more significant number of customers. The SWOT analysis for this initiative is:

- Strength – Employee optimism is high. Organisation's market share has increased.
- Weaknesses – Lack of strategic customer management system. Monthly customer engagement numbers have fallen.
- Opportunity – Demand for customers the organisation is dealing with has increased monthly. Rising number of customers using digital tools has increased.
- Threats – Low value of products offered by the organisation. Negative impact on enviroment due to paper printing.

You need to understand **why** an enterprise needs to change some aspect of its operations and what would be directly or indirectly affected by the change.

Business analysts need to:

- focus on outcomes required to be achieved by planning and defining an agenda
- have a clear understanding of the business context

- have a clear view of any internal and external environments to fully understand the scope of the transformation
- elaborate on business needs and outcomes.

Strategy analysis is essential as it supports the decision-making process. It provides information about the evaluation, development of the environment, and anything else that may impact internal and external factors of the organisation.

The BABOK® Guide is an area of knowledge in which business analysts collaborate with stakeholders to elaborate on a need for strategic or tactical importance. Keeping in mind that the *strategic* outlines what needs to be achieved from an organisational point of view, whilst *tactical* is about how to try and achieve it. As identified in the second point above, I would like to highlight the importance of needing to address enterprise-wide needs and aligning them with organisational objectives.

The activities could include:

- An analysis of current state by understanding the company's operating model.
- Identifying future state by clearly identifying business goals and objectives, and ensuring they are aligned with the business needs.
- Clearly articulating what parts of the company need to change.
- Some standard techniques to effectively capture the current and future state are using business process maps. Some companies may already have well-defined business process maps (at required levels). I strongly recommend creating process maps for the current and future conditions if you cannot get your hands on a current state map.

Mind maps are valuable for initial brainstorming to clarify topics, and visually represent problem-solving and decision-making. They support:

- assessing any risks and uncertainties resulting from the proposed change

- identifying the change strategy by carrying out a gap analysis between the current and future state.

3. Elicitation and collaboration

To conduct practical requirements elicitation and collaboration, business analysts must spend time preparing and understanding the scope of the required elicitation activities, selecting appropriate techniques, planning workshops and reviewing supporting materials and resources. During requirements elicitation, business analysts need to communicate and collaborate with the key stakeholders to gain insights and identify needs.

Requirements elicitation encompasses research and the discovery of user and customer needs (requirements) of a specific stakeholder.

This phase is collaboration-heavy and can be complex as you need to call out challenges you are trying to resolve and understand your customers' needs. You need to ensure the requirements elicitation is completed and clear. This will ensure what gets delivered meets customer needs, and preparation for this is key. There is further information on the deliverables related to requirements in the Key deliverables section of this chapter.

Use the following questions to ask the right questions when eliciting requirements and collaborating with your stakeholders. They are divided into questions to assess current state, future state and stakeholders. Use columns Yes and No to keep a track of the questions you have asked.

Activity 5.1. Right questions for current state

Question	Yes	No
1. What are the current business activities?		
2. Who are these activities being performed by?		
3. What is the information flow?		
4. What are the inputs and outputs?		
5. What are the impacts on people, processes and technology?		
6. What information is missing?		
7. What are the current problems in the process or with the current information?		
8. What is working well and should not be changed?		
9. What would happen if this activity were removed?		
10. When is the activity complete?		
11. Where does the process start?		
12. Where does the process finish?		
13. Where does the activity occur?		

Activity 5.2. Right questions for future state

Question	Yes	No
1. What queries or reports will be needed?		
2. What should future business activities be?		
3. Should this activity be manual or automated?		
4. What should the inputs and outputs be?		
5. What types of information will be needed?		
6. What should the information flow be?		
7. What should the end state be?		
8. What reports can be removed?		
9. Where should this information be stored?		
10. Where should the process start?		
11. Where should the process finish?		
12. Where should the activity occur?		
13. Who should the activities be performed by?		
14. When should the activity be done?		
15. How should the activities be performed in the future?		
16. Why is the activity required?		

Activity 5.3. Right questions to collaborate with stakeholders

Question	Yes	No
1. Who are the different stakeholders who will impact or be affected by this change?		
2. Who can be a key contact point for communication and effectively represent this group?		
3. Why will they care about this change, i.e., what is their stake in the outcome?		
4. What do the stakeholders need?		
5. Which actions will best meet the stakeholders' needs?		
6. What will the impact be?		
7. What do you believe people need to know and understand for the change to be made easily and quickly?		
8. What are people expecting, and what are their key concerns about the change?		
9. What other changes or business activities are occurring that we need to be aware of and accommodate when planning communications and training for this program or project?		
10. What forms of engagement and communication work well for your organisation and/or stakeholders, and what should we avoid when garnering awareness, understanding and commitment to the change?		

Effective requirements elicitation and collaboration

To ensure requirements are effectively captured, you need to:

- be well prepared – have a plan with clear objectives
- have the correct stakeholder and domain knowledge in the room
- send out well-prepared packs with detailed information (background, reference material, etc.) to get the message across
- gain a commitment on the ownership of who will prepare the meeting minutes and action items
- have all the admin set-up (physical or virtual) done and prepared in advance.

4. Requirements management

A requirement is something that a business needs and define what the business will achieve. Once we know what our requirements are, we need to manage them.

Requirements management encompasses analysing, documenting, validating, prioritising, agreeing to and approving requirements, managing change and communicating to applicable stakeholders and team members. Requirements management is an ongoing process throughout a project.

Business analysts will dive deep into the requirements, ensuring there are enough details for developers to develop (customise or configure) a desired solution, and testers to test against detailed requirements.

The requirements deliverable at this level is functional (aka solution requirements). In this deliverable, the requirements are further elaborated on and used in user stories that contain acceptance criteria or use case format. It is important to include business rules and, in some cases, data, validation rules and data descriptions (for example, for technical interface requirements). And create mock-ups (where appropriate). Sometimes you may be asked to produce more specialised requirements, such as interface requirements or data migration requirements.

Prioritisation activity is also an essential part of requirements management. Usually business analysts will work closely with critical stakeholders, product owners and delivery leads to collectively prioritise requirements.

Don't forget to complete the *to-be* business processes, which most often need to be completed to level 6 (enough for the training and working instructions to be produced). Lately, the projects I've been working on have used using BPMN (Business Process Model and Notation), a commonly used standard to create business process maps.

A crucial part of a business analyst's role is to continually update and validate the functional (aka solution) requirements until these are signed off. You may even need to update the applicable requirements later in a project, such as delivery. It is essential to keep track of changes and raise change requests (as per the process you might be following in your organisation).

Effective requirements management

Requirements can generally change as more information and knowledge are captured while working with stakeholders and SMEs, particularly during the deep solution dive. Periodically stakeholders may change their minds around specific requirements. The trick is to know how to manage the changes and ensure when to lock down the requirements. Conditions need to be managed proactively in anticipation of change. This is where Agile methodology plays a big part in working closely with stakeholders and understanding their needs.

The following are some tips on how to manage requirements effectively:

- ensure requirements are well defined
- conduct requirements walkthroughs with stakeholders
- make sure you communicate often and clearly throughout the project, and that any proposed changes are communicated to all parties
- prioritise requirements by considering benefits, risks, dependency, feasibility and perhaps using the MOSCOW technique to identify

high, medium or low risks or the desirable, must-have or critical, must, should, could priority of requirements.

After conducting many interviews, I have realised that focusing on the following essential questions are helpful in eliciting the information needed:

- What?
- When?
- Where?
- Who?
- How?
- Why?

Before going to an interview, I always write these key questions down and categorise them. I have found that preparing for the discussions this way makes the interview easier to follow and ensures that the required information is captured. Additionally, preparing a list helps me ensure that the right questions and situations are played out in interviews.

Use the following to ask the right questions when eliciting business requirements.

Activity 5.4. Right questions when eliciting requirements

Question	Yes	No
1. Who should I talk to to learn more about this?		
2. Who are the reports produced for? Is any additional information required?		
3. How will their involvement in the project be managed?		
4. How should the new feature be used?		
5. How will it change the work in process?		
6. How should we meet this business need?		
7. How will we know this is complete?		
8. How will stakeholder involvement in the program or project be managed?		
9. How are we going to accommodate the migration?		
10. Who is impacted by this effort?		
11. Who is sponsoring this effort?		
12. Who are the SMEs?		
13. Where should the user be located physically when using this feature?		
14. Where should the user access this feature?		
15. Where does the process start?		
16. Where should the results be visible?		
17. When will this feature be used?		
18. When do you need to know about the feature?		

Question	Yes	No
19. When will the feature fail?		
20. When will we be ready to start?		
21. Who should use this feature?		
22. Who should deliver the inputs for the feature?		
23. Who should receive the outputs of the feature?		
24. Who should learn about the results of someone using this feature?		
25. What areas do they represent?		
26. What does the new system look and feel like?		
27. What is the system?		
28. What are the features of the system?		
29. What assumptions are being made about this feature?		
30. What does this feature need to do?		
31. What is the result of doing this?		
32. What needs to happen next?		
33. What must happen before this feature?		
34. What if? Think of all the alternative scenarios. Make sure you ask about what should happen if those scenarios play out.		
35. What is the mapping of the new fields (if known)?		
36. Is the way the data is structured in the old system the same as in the new designs?		

Question	Yes	No
37. What are the existing business rules for the old product and new product?		
38. What are the impacts on processes, people and technology?		
39. What are reports requirements internally and externally?		
40. What additional reports are required to be produced?		
41. Is there any other way to accomplish this?		
42. Does this feature meet the business's need and solve the problem we're trying to solve?		

Why questions will assist in confirming that the requirements elicited map back to a need to be identified in the project's scope.

Verifying requirements ensures that the needs and designs have been defined correctly. Requirements verification constitutes a check by the business analyst and key stakeholders to determine that the requirements and procedures are ready for validation, and provides the information needed for further work.

A high-quality specification is well-written and easily understood by its intended audience. A high-quality model follows notation standards and effectively represents reality.

5. Skills and techniques

Here are the skills that I consider essential to being a good business analyst, to be part of the best business analysis team, and to support successful requirements analysis and design, as well as complementary skills also required to support the core skill set.

Analytical thinking and problem-solving

This is an essential core skill set for every business analyst to possess. An analytical mindset and problem-solving skills are needed to effectively analyse problem areas, and search for and propose opportunities for improvements that deliver the most value. Business analysts will need to use substantial amounts of information and data to learn and effectively identify future improvements.

Behavioural characteristics

Possessing behavioural characteristics such as making ethical decisions, being accountable, trustworthiness, being organised, time management and adaptability are essential for business analysts. Understanding the different behaviours of our stakeholders and team members is as crucial in order to create trust and understand organisational and project dynamics. For example, your stakeholder likes to be listened to, particularly if there are opposite points of view. Ensure you regularly communicate with them and be an active listener to build trust. Another stakeholder may prefer visual representations when working with them and eliciting requirements. Show them you care and produce more visual diagrams to capture and support their needs.

Business knowledge

I have found that business knowledge helps deliver quality business requirements in the finance and superannuation industries. Business knowledge is required to assist business analysts in better understanding the concepts discussed and in analysing the benefits and values to be achieved.

Additionally, industry, mobile and digital knowledge are also important.

Industry knowledge

Industry knowledge is essential as it provides the business analyst with an understanding of existing practices and activities, current market trends, key processes, service offerings, product disclosures, industry best practices and regulations. While working in the financial and superannuation sectors, I have discovered the importance of industry knowledge and standards. Each industry is different and complex due to variations in products, service offerings, regulations and the parties involved.

Mobile and digital knowledge
In this age, it is important for a business analyst to understand and know digital and mobile ways of working. With a traditional approach, business analysts focused mainly on internal stakeholders. These days, you will be just as focused on the external outputs and stakeholders of an organisation. And let's face it, most things these days involve mobile technology, from banking to checking your superannuation fund. So, knowledge in this area is important.

Communication skills

Business analysts are required to be competent in their verbal, non-verbal, and written communication and listening skills. These skills are essential to be successful in our roles as facilitators, problem-solvers and value creators.

Written and verbal communication
As business analysts, we are required to translate and communicate ideas and concept options to various stakeholders, verbally and in written deliverables. You may need to run a workshop, for example, addressing stakeholders verbally and presenting in PowerPoint. Clarity and engagement in communication are essential to these activities.

Active listening
Active listening is another important communication skill as it helps us to further understand our stakeholders, at different levels, and builds trust and rapport with them.

Interpersonal skills

Interpersonal skills assist business analysts in communicating and collaborating effectively with customers or stakeholders (including senior stakeholders). You may need to interact with sponsors at executive levels, change teams, vendors, developers and team members. As a business analyst you are required to facilitate, provide business analysis leadership, and encourage understanding of value with the interactions you are required to have.

Tools and technology

You will be required to use a variety of different methods and software to support communication, collaboration, analysis and project delivery. Some commonly used options to document elicited requirements are:

- Jira
- Confluence
- Google Docs
- Google Sheets
- PowerPoint
- MS Word
- MS Project (for BA plans)
- MS Excel
- MS Teams, Zoom, Google Meet, Skype, GoTo Meeting
- MS Visio
- Post-its
- SharePoint
- Slack
- murals, physical rooms or a combination.

Lately, I have mainly been using Confluence as a document repository to capture BRDs including reference(s) to the process maps (for example, process maps might be created from MS Visio, if no other process mapping tool is available), and linkages to dependencies or assumptions (these may potentially sit in a location in Jira, etc.).

Complementary core skills

To perform as a good business analyst you need to possess these underscoring, complementary skills. The complementary skills outlined are further described in detail in the BABOK® Guide.

Trustworthiness

Earning the trust of stakeholders helps business analysts elicit business analysis information around sensitive issues and enables us to help stakeholders have confidence that our recommendations will be adequately and fairly evaluated. Be honest. Display confidence and garner trust in everything you do.

Adaptability

As a business analyst, you will often be working with different stakeholders and changing environments and specifications. You must adjust your procedural approach and how you interact with different stakeholders in certain situations. I have found myself having to be mindful and ask varying questions when moving between different industries.

For example, I ran workshops for the dairy industry and regulators as I needed to elicit business (stakeholder) requirements. My initial preparation for the workshop encompassed research in what information is available on internet and what my project team had access to. I familiarised myself with terminology they might be using and how their teams might be operating. I quickly learnt to understand compliance requirements, such as milk storage temperatures.

The way I ran the workshop is by having well-prepared questions to ask (including using the terminology of their industry). Additionally, I would start by playing back to them my understanding of the framework, their industry, etc., and walk through process maps of their team's operating model.

Requirements statements

Requirements statements are deliverables from requirements elicitation sessions. These can be identified in the form of user stories or statements, during the initiation stage of a project or initiative, known as stakeholder or business requirements (I usually refer to these as high-level requirements). See the Key deliverables section on key deliverables elaborated further to learn more.

Personal ownership and accountability

As business analysts, we need to have accountability in completing business analysis tasks on time, setting expectations for stakeholders and team members, and ensure that we meet those expectations.

Creative thinking

Creative thinking is an essential underlying skill to have. It allows us to look at a problem from a different perspective, and come up with new ideas and concepts. Not everyone is naturally a creative thinker. You can improve your creative thinking mindset by going out there, meeting new people that may challenge your assumptions, actively try to do something new, such as learn a new skill, explore music and art.

Visual and conceptual thinking

Conceptual thinking (as described in detail in a Guide to the Business Analysis Body of Knowledge (BABOK® Guide)) is about working through the linkage between contexts, solutions, needs, value, changes and stakeholders.

Visual representations are a great way to provide a graphic representation of the specific needs, opinions or systems being elaborated on.

Visual and conceptual thinking supports analytical thinking and problem-solving.

Decision-making

The decision-making process encompasses using the available information and guiding stakeholders, critical decision-making, analysing, comparing options and using the information gathered to ultimately make a decision.

Learning

"The more that you read, the more things you will know.
The more that you learn, the more places you will go."
—Dr. Seuss"[9]

Solution knowledge

Having solution knowledge is useful as business analysts draw on our knowledge and experience we have in the requirements gathering of the solution improvements. Understanding off-the-shelf commercial solutions will also assist you when seeking possible solutions.

Network and infrastructure

Business analysts may sometimes be allocated to network and infrastructure projects, to perform a deep dive technical analysis. Understanding network and infrastructure are beneficial when you are required to deliver technical analysis in this space. Businesses investing in secure network infrastructure and modern technology (like cloud or Azure) are only as reliable as the cabling they run on. I have been engaged across many lifecycle projects, for example, where operating systems need to be upgraded to new versions, such as Windows 7.0 to Windows 10.

Body language mindfulness

Since the most important part of a business analyst's world is communication, body language can provide the foundation for even deeper communication. I read the body movements, facial expressions, eye contact and human behavioural information of my clients. Being aware of body

9 Dr Seuss, *I can read with my eyes shut!*, Random House UK, 1978.

language in others is important for making judgements about their level of comfort and what they might be thinking or expecting.

Facilitation and teamwork

Facilitation and teamwork are important assets for business analysts. When facilitating, business analysts use our interpersonal skills to identify and assess problems, exchange information and ideas, understand requirements and gain approval. Business analysts work closely with our team members to translate requirements testing, development or change. Business analysts may work in a group, facilitating requirements to capture these collectively. So working effectively together in a team is vital.

Negotiation and conflict resolution

Negotiation and conflict resolution skills come in handy when having to negotiate requirements, and also when dealing with conflicting opinions. By having strong negotiation and conflict resolution skills, you will be able to come to a compromise for all parties involved effectively. I have been on many projects where different stakeholders had opposing opinions on requirements and priorities. By seeing two or more sides and finding common ground, I use persuasion and planning to help reach a compromise and keep moving the project forward.

Techniques

To get the knowledge areas right, business analysts need to be competent in the following techniques:

- business analysis planning and monitoring
- strategic analysis
- elicitation and collaboration
- requirements management.

Business analysis planning and monitoring

A critical aspect of any project or initiative is to spend quality time planning. The planning phase is essential. Over the years, I've seen business analysts getting increasingly involved at a strategy level, understanding the goals, objectives and values projects are trying to deliver, and planning is a key part to that.

Business analysis plans include:

- activities
- level of details
- templates (e.g., BRD documents or user stories)
- dates key requirements are to be signed off.

Some tools you may choose to assist with planning are a Gantt chart (MS Project), Post-it notes or MS Excel.

Strategic analysis

Brainstorming

This method can encourage thinking about a problem, discussing ideas and identifying where further analysis is required.

Business analysts should use brainstorming to gather ideas, elaborate on topics and discuss and create solutions for stakeholders in a short period of time. Using the brainstorming technique, you could generate innovative ideas with your stakeholders.

This is used to collaboratively identify and reach a consensus about which sources of business analysis information should be captured and which elicitation techniques might be most effective.

Document analysis

This technique involves finding the documents that are available to you, such as user manuals, software vendor manuals and process documents. These documents can provide the inputs for the new system requirements. They are particularly useful in understanding or completing the *as-is* process document and conducting gap analysis for scoping the project.

- *Mind mapping*

A visual technique used to find patterns and relationships amongst ideas. For example, come up with a keyword or phrase by putting it in the middle of a page, then write down ideas and details regarding the main topic and draw some lines around it.

- *Process mapping*

Process mapping is a great visual representation of the sequence of steps within a business process. It is most useful when exploring the current state and working out what the to-be state needs to be.

Business process mapping is the visual display of the steps within a business process showing how it's done from the start to finish. This mapping provides a concise picture of the steps needed to deliver a product, service or other processes from start to finish.

- *SWOT analysis*

One of the practical techniques you could use is SWOT analysis (strengths, weaknesses, opportunities, threats). A SWOT analysis is generally used to understand the overall state of a specific organisation (internally and externally).

Elicitation and collaboration

Interviews

An interview is a systematic approach to elicit information from a person or group. In this case, the business analyst acts as an interviewer, providing an opportunity to explore and understand needs and requirements in more detail. Without knowing the expectations and goals of the stakeholders, it isn't easy to fulfil requirements.

Interviews are used to identify concerns about the planned elicitation and can be used to seek authority to proceed with specific options. You can use the lists of questions in this book to shape your interviews.

Workshops
This is an excellent way of getting everybody together to define the scope and identify and prioritise requirements.

Workshops comprise a group of users or stakeholders working together to identify requirements in a structured way. Workshops are used to scope, discover, define and prioritise needs for the proposed system. They are an effective way to deliver high-quality requirements quickly. They promote mutual understanding and strong communication between stakeholders, customers and the project team.

Planned meetings
As part of my planning for the elicitation and collaboration phase, I spend time defining what sessions I need to have, when and how, and who needs to be involved. My plan usually includes:

- workshop date(s)
- timeframes and durations
- a clear agenda
- reading materials that I ask participants to read before the sessions
- assessing the business domain (domain knowledge experts) and stakeholders (required to be engaged to get the right information)
- clearly articulated goals, objectives, outcomes
- setting expectations on who owns documentation.

Make sure you prepare the audience by setting the right expectations of what is required from them. You need to seek buy-in on the proposed plan and the process that you will share.

Workshop meeting invites are sent out as placeholder meetings in participants' calendars. I usually send an email explaining the expectations and agreeing on the meeting minute taker's responsibility. Additionally, I validate my list with the senior project sponsor and project manager to ensure appropriate stakeholders are involved and nothing has been missed.

Here are some tips for the types of preparation you will need to carry out for meetings and workshops:

- *Before the meeting*

What is the goal? What is the client's purpose? Prepare what message you would like to get across and what you would like to achieve together, what essential requirements you are planning to capture, etc.

- *During the meeting*

Clearly articulate the purpose, ask the client and/or stakeholders their points of view, discuss alternatives, next steps and any consequences of not capturing the requirements.

- *After the meeting*

Check in and see if the message captured in the meeting is correct. By the check-in you will re-evaluate their trust in you, and your ability to understand and capture their needs.

Unplanned meetings

You can also have unplanned meetings to assist with requirements gathering, such as last-minute or 'in the nick of time' collaboration or conversations.

Business analysis information captured from an unplanned activity may need more detailed exploration during a future planned activity.

Surveys or questionnaires

You can collect information using a questionnaire, which are helpful when a lot of information needs to be gathered from a larger group of stakeholders. This enables the business team to gather requirements from stakeholders remotely without needing a meeting. The questions need to be designed so that they do not influence the answers you will receive. You may want to engage someone that specialises in this area.

Observations

The observation technique is useful for business analysts to gain information while watching and understanding workplace activities. Business analysts may observe the business processes within the scope of the project. This is something that you will need to negotiate with your client.

Customer journey

The customer journey is **a series of customer experiences over a period that results in a business outcome**. The customer journey is underpinned by the customer's emotional state that characterises an experience, being primarily positive or negative. Plotting or brainstorming customer journeys (using a type of process map, with a particular emphasis on seeing things from the customer's perspective) is an effective way of walking in a customer's shoes.

Why is the customer journey important?

"*Human beings are emotional creatures and research has shown the emotion has a huge influence on our memory, motivation, and behaviour. Emotion is a strong correlate to rooting an experience deep in ones physic and providing that association between customer and organisation.*"[10]

Fishbeck explains how good experiences can make up for good emotions and an organisation can this into account and give a customer an experience that will make them feel better.

I find a huge benefit as part of the business requirements management phase to be able to influence and understand their emotional experience. As the saying goes, walk-in the customers' shoes.

Requirements management

Backlog groom

A regular session in which backlog items are discussed, reviewed and prioritised by product owners, product managers and other members of the team. The aim is to ensure backlog (user stories, tasks) is kept up to date and is ready for any upcoming sprints.

10 M Fishbeck, 'Customer Journey Mapping for Business Analysts', modernanalysts.com, accessed 15 February 2023.

User stories
Business analysts can deliver requirements in a user story format, particularly when working in Agile or hybrid environments. The greatest benefit I find in delivering conditional user stories is ensuring that a need satisfies desired value. These are usually written by business analysts or customers and product owners. The product owners can manage these user stories in the backlog and prioritise them as required.

Prototyping
Business analysts can validate the requirements (use cases, business rules, scenarios) against a developed solution using this method. By creating and designing the requirements through an repetitive processes, BAs are able to elicit and validate identified requirements. Additionally, prototypes can be used to assess design options, improve user experience and simulate the final business solution.

Screen mock-ups
Screen mock-ups can support the requirement gathering process when introduced at the correct time. Mock-ups help stakeholders visualise the functionality of a system. This can be an advantage to business analysts and stakeholders since this allows them to identify gaps or problems early on.

Joint Application Development
The Joint Application Development (JAD) technique can be used following a workshop. When running the JAD session, stakeholders and the project team work together to identify the requirements. These sessions are efficient as they allow the business team to gather and consolidate large amounts of information.

Data mining
This is used to identify information or patterns requiring further investigation.

Fit gap analysis

In fit gap analysis, the business analysts identify processes and outcomes, comparing them to the ideal outcomes and working on the plan for changes to be made in systems. A fit gap analysis can be tricky as it can be challenging to develop the ideal outcomes and steps to achieve these outcomes.

Data modelling

Data modelling is useful to provide a visual representation of a whole information system or a certain part to communicate data points, relationships and structures. When working more on technical documentation, these are commonly used and may need you to compile a technical or interface document.

In addition to the techniques discussed above, there are many more on the market. You will need to work with your stakeholder, understanding the nature of your project and organisation structure, and as a team find out what suits your group best. In my work settings, I've mainly used brainstorming, document analysis, interviews, prototyping, data mapping and workshops.

Key deliverables

Let's talk about requirements deliverables. The key deliverables from the business analysis perspective are the elaborated and documented requirements, (including solution recommendation) that deliver value to stakeholders.

The requirement types and key deliverables you may be required to carry out include:

- business or stakeholder requirements, aka high-level requirements, or HLRs
- functional, detailed level requirements (DLRs), aka solution requirements
- non-functional requirements (NFRs)
- a requirements traceability matrix (RTM).

Requirements can be documented and categorised at different stages of a project, and varying levels of detail requirements should start with the context of the business, its processes and clearly defined business needs. Requirements identify the gaps between the current and future state analysis and enable companies to achieve the future state.

Please note that the requirements categorisation varies under different methodologies, such as Waterfall and Agile. You will find that the requirement's classification or naming convention has changed over the years based on the methodology used. However, the primary classification of conditions remains unchanged.

Business or stakeholder requirements

Business requirements (also referred to as high-level business requirements, or HLBR) describe what the solution must provide to fulfil the *to-be* enterprise architecture, objectives, outputs and outcomes. The business requirements are based on what has been outlined in the business case. Business analysts must ensure enough detail has been documented to support the planning and estimation activities while considering the best, most likely or worst-case scenarios.

Functional or solution requirements

Functional or solution requirements (aka detail level business requirements, or DLBR) are defined as part of the IIBA industry standard in the BABOK® Guide. These are stakeholder requirements typically captured along with business requirements. A solution requirements document describes the needs of a particular stakeholder or class of stakeholders.

Detailed requirements contain the elaborated requirements to support downstream design, build and testing execution. The functional requirements define what the solution must do. The functional requirements stipulate what the user should be able to do with the solution. The functional requirements can be represented in the form of user cases. The template will depend on the company you are working for. For most projects I've worked on, functional requirements have been documented using user cases, including the specification of acceptance criteria and scenarios.

"The key to a good requirement(s) is that the requirement MUST be clear enough (not ambiguous) and understood by anyone (including stakeholders, developers, testers etc.). You need to ensure enough requirement(s) are documented to assist with successful project delivery."
—Maria Montgomery [11]

Non-functional requirements (NFRs)

NFRs (also known as quality of service) are quality attributes that a solution must have or be. NFRs identify the quality and behavioural characteristics of a solution. These requirements must be aligned with how the service levels of the system are measured and reported to the stakeholders. The NFRs should include users (and the number of users), security, usability, accessibility, compliance, regulatory, legal, privacy, confidentiality, extensibility, scalability, adaptability, configurability, customer experience, audit ability and operational performance.

NFRs should also include:

- **quality requirements** that identify testable quality expectations of the system or business, for example, the system must process a payment in less than three seconds, on average
- **service level requirements** are business requirements that identify performance over time. For instance, the solution will be available 99.94% of the time.

From experience, most projects already have NFRs predefined and available for you to update. However, I've worked on projects where I had to develop the NFRs from scratch. The NFRs can be written either in a separate section of the detailed requirements document or a separate NFRs document. It makes sense to have a separate NFR document when making updates for different releases on an extensive program of work.

11 M Montgomery, 'The art of tailoring to project methodologies and templates to deliver effective / concise requirements on your projectmedium.com', medium.com, 17 May 2020, accessed 5 February 2023.

Additionally, information security is extremely important as it protects sensitive information from unauthorised activities (anything that looks suspicious) that needs investigation, modification and recording. This reminds me of the huge cyber-attack on Optus in 2022 and customer information being exposed.

I remember leading the activity of non-functional requirements centralisation for my company as we did not have a centralised NFR repository at the time. BAs did not have a way finding any existing NFRs, and only a few projects captured ad hoc NFRs. I have proposed to the senior leadership team to create and lead a new initiative to centralise NFRs. This initiative was quickly approved as our organisation understood the benefits of this initiative. Kirsten (Lead Business Analyst at the time) and I created a plan and ran workshops across a whole organisation to create and gain an agreement.

Understanding the fact that the key stakeholder needed to be on board in owning and understanding a need for a centralised repository, a decision was made to start with ten key standard non-functional requirements.

- **Availability:** the degree to which the solution is operable and accessible when required for use, often expressed in terms of the percentage of time the solution is available.
- **Compatibility:** the degree to which the solution operates effectively with other components in its environment, such as one process interacting with another.
- **Maintainability:** the ease with which a solution or component can be modified to correct faults, improve performance or other attributes, or adapt to a changing environment.
- **Performance efficiency:** the degree to which a solution or component performs its designated functions with minimum consumption of resources. It can be defined based on the context or period, such as high-peak, mid-peak or off-peak usage.
- **Portability:** the ease with which a solution or component can be transferred from one environment to another.
- **Scalability:** the degree to which a solution can grow or evolve to handle increased amounts of work or traffic.

- **Security:** aspects of a solution that protect solution content or solution components from accidental or malicious access, use, modification, destruction or disclosure.
- **Usability:** the ease with which a user can learn to use the solution.
- **Compliance:** regulatory, financial or legal constraints that can vary based on the context or jurisdiction.
- **Service level agreements:** constraints of the organisation being served by the solution that is formally agreed to by both the provider and the user of the solution.

Once Kirsten and I identified the key non-functional requirements, the RASCI for each was established and agreed on by the senior leadership team. **RASCI** is important in identifying ownership for NFRs and it stands for:

Responsible – Identifying who needs to make sure the NFRs are an accurate representation of a need.

Accountable – Who has ultimate control over the NFR and its resources.

Support – Who will provide help to the responsible individual.

Consulted – Who will give advice to the responsible individual.

Informed – Who needs to be kept in the loop during identification, approvals or any updates.

Once an agreement on the NFRs and ownership was established, a centralised repository and governance process to ensure NFRs continued to stay current was created. The initiative took at least two months to achieve, however, it was a beneficial outcome. I see a great need and place for NFRs, and I have written more on NFRs in this article.

Additionally, another initiative initiated by the BA team was the centralisation of business (stakeholder), functional (solutions) requirements. We needed to have a centralised repository of all requirements captured across the organisation for the BAs to have easy access to existing documentation and reduce rework (where appropriate).

The centralisation of the business was led by another amazing Lead Business Analyst, Wendy Loo, where the requirements were shared across the BA community. This led to high-quality requirements packages that can be used across different projects and are useful to both stakeholders and developers. The community that started with three business analysts ended up with more than thirty members at one point.

Requirements traceability matrix (RTM)

A requirements traceability matrix (RTM) is produced but not necessarily owned by business analysts. Usually, business analysts are required to facilitate the completion of the RTM. All requirements must be traced to the design, process and test cases to ensure coverage (and that everything is delivered as expected).

The purpose of the RTM is to delineate the relationship between requirements and other related artefacts. Its key goal is to prove that conditions have been fulfilled, requirements have been tested and test results and issues have been documented. Currently, some tools could potentially provide automated RTMs, for example, Jira, Confluence and X-ray.

The maintenance of requirements is important as it allows the retention of requirement accuracy, and consistency throughout and beyond the change during the entire requirements lifecycle. It is there to support the reuse of requirements in other solutions.

KEY TAKEAWAYS

- If you are setting up a business analysis practice, developing competency and professional development plans, you need to continuously conduct audits of members' competency and skills. Skills-sharing is also imperative as it allows the exchange of knowledge. It assists with new approaches to a successful outcome.
- You need to have a deep understanding and knowledge in all five knowledge areas:
  1. business analysis planning and monitoring
  2. strategy analysis
  3. elicitation and collaboration
  4. requirements management, encompasses requirements deliverables and requirements lifecycle management

5. skills and techniques encompass skills essential by BAs and techniques BAs need to be competent.

- Make sure you are well prepared and ask the right questions when undertaking eliciting and validating requirements.
- Ensure requirements are effectively captured, always be well prepared.
- Don't forget the complementary skill sets. You need to be clear on these as they support the core competency skill set.

ACTION YOU CAN TAKE

- Refer to you Knowledge Audit (Activity 3.1: Knowledge audit template) in Chapter 3. Further re-assess your knowledge against the five knowledge areas covered in this chapter.
- Keep *Activity 4.1: So, what does it take to do well checklist* handy to refer to when you are assessing your knowledge areas.
- Use *Activity 5.1: Right questions for current state*, *Activity 5.3: Right questions to collaborate with stakeholders*, *Activity 5.4: Right questions when eliciting requirements* to ensure you are well prepared when eliciting requirements.

PART 3

Leadership that builds the best business analysts and BA practice

To be successful in the business analysis world you need to provide strong leadership in building and supporting the best BA team and practice.

Chapter 6 covers building a strong, well-developed practice and the importance of having a business analysis community to succeed.

Chapter 7 looks at how to be a good business analyst and some of the core competencies to maintain your capacity, and that of your team.

Chapter 6

Business analysis practice and community

"Alone, we do so little; together, we can do so much."
—Helen Keller [12]

12 H Keller, *The Story of My Life*, Dover Publications Inc, 2000.

As a leader, to have a successful business analysis team, you need to **ensure a business analysis community of practice is set up**. A business analysis community of practice (COP) is important to getting it right as it brings individuals together to share ideas and best practice with each other. It is great for individuals to come together and learn how to do it better. Setting up a business analysis practice within your organisation is beneficial. The practice will assist with understanding the gaps in knowledge and training needs. A practice facilitates innovation and knowledge sharing, and this leads to higher quality output, more consistently.

I led the team of business analysts at UniSuper in creating the business analysis community of practice. I started with three enthusiastic business analysts, looking for a community to share ideas, knowledge and professional development. I began setting up fortnightly meetings to discuss a topic of interest and gaps in practice, such as templates and guidelines required to assist us in getting business analysis right.

During our discovery, a Kanban board was created that encompassed initiatives that were then prioritised. I sought volunteers to lead and finalise each initiative. The steps were to:

- create a business analysis framework, which included our mission, objectives and goals, to be shared with rest of the organisation
- develop and populate the Kanban board with prioritised initiatives to achieve by the end of year
- assign volunteers to each initiative, including a leader to lead the outcomes and plan the actions for each initiative
- communicate to the rest of the organisations about the purpose of our BA COP
- share deliverables from each initiative across the organisation through Yammer (our organisation group chat), lunch and learn sessions and showcase sessions
- invite guess speakers from various business units to present a topic of interest (for example, security and enterprise architecture)
- connecting with other teams to find better ways of working (for example, our change partners and security architects)

- adjusting and creating various templates that will work with our internal teams and provide quality requirements.

As a leader that created this business analysis community of practice, I am very proud that UniSuper had our business analysis practice chosen as a finalist for the IIBA Business Analysis Practice of the Year Awards in 2022. This is a proven example that bringing people together who share the same passion for what they do, learn and achieve can result in great outcomes.

Building the best business analysis practice

As articulated by Kathleen B Hass, to build best business analysis practice, the following elements are must haves:

- *"An acknowledgement of the value of business analysis as a critical business practice*
- *A competent BA workforce*
- *Effective business analysis methods, tools and support*
- *A BA centre of excellence that establishes and maintains the practice."*

—*Kathleen B Hass*[13]

I have found Kathleen provides a great description and a diagram on how elements to build a mature practice fit in the overall practice. For more details refer to the further reading, and Kathleen's book *The enterprise business analyst*.

Build the best team and be a good leader

As a leader building a BA team, don't be afraid to roll your sleeves up and help your team get the work done. I remember when I was a Lead Business Analyst when the Agile methodology had just been introduced and

13 KB Hass, 'The enterprise Business Analyst: Developing Creative Solutions to Complex Business Problems', Berrett-Koehler Publishers, 1 September 2011.

my project was doing a pilot. We began with four-week iterations, and had principles and guidelines established to measure the success and outcomes by the team.

I remember a day when my team (including me) was asked to perform testing due to the unavailability of the testing environments and services provided by our testing partners working from India. I was told that all systems were down overseas, hence no testing was completed, and our work was nearing the last days of a sprint. I ended up helping my team with the testing myself. That day I was a Lead, a Senior Business Analyst and a business analyst. You need to do everything you can to help your team, to ensure deliverables are completed on time and to a high standard.

How to recruit the right people

To support the right competencies, you need to recruit right people. To get the right candidate for the job, I recommend:

- Have a thorough and descriptive job description. Make sure people know what they are applying for. Include any specific criteria you would like them to meet (such as industry experience, specific application experience, etc.).
- Question candidates to determine how their inspiration, drivers and goals align with the tasks you need them to perform.
- Consider evaluation strategies beyond the face-to-face interview. Identify a set of criteria that you assess each candidate against.
- Pay attention to the questions they ask.
- Prepare well-structured questions to ask in your interview.
- Tap into your network and individuals you have worked with in the past, as you will be familiar with their capabilities. This will make it easier for you to assess whether they could work well in your team.

During interviews, make sure you ask questions such as "What are your weaknesses?" as it encourages candidates to articulate areas where they lack tangible skills. It will provide you with an insight into which areas the candidates might be developing in, or if they are proactive in their professional development.

Hire someone you could work for if the roles were reversed. And take your time.

Have someone in the interview with you. Get their point of view. Go back and reflect on the notes you may have taken. Be clear about your expectations.

Being clear upfront provides transparency and honesty. If your candidates drop off, that is not necessarily a bad thing; it could mean that people are no longer interested in the job because it is not the right fit for them. And always trust your instincts.

Review the job description, and then structure your questions to align to with it. Make sure you include some questions to uncover a candidate's interpersonal skills. Some of my favourite questions are:

- What gets you up in the morning?
- How do you like to be managed?
- What are your activities outside of work? Any side projects?
- What are your key achievements outside of work?

And lastly, don't forget to check their profiles on social media, such as Facebook, Instagram and LinkedIn. Check who they relate to. Many times, I've found someone that may have worked with the candidate so I can follow up to see if they have any feedback on them. See if your network can deliver some assistance.

When it comes to working with and leading your team, you need to be open-minded, listen to your team members and try to compromise. For example, sometimes you *need* to assign a team member to a project that will not help them achieve their goals; the work needs to be done after all. However, if your team has seen that you have a track record of helping with their development goals, you can have a transparent conversation with your team member and assure them you will re-assign them as soon as you possibly can. If possible, plan what the next step will be. So, it's a give and take. Ensure that they get the opportunity to work on the projects they wish to work on, if not now, maybe in the future. Talk to your team members and create a plan together. I've found actively listening to my team members has helped me grow trust and build strong teams that deliver the right outcomes. I have had feedback that they liked working with me. I'm great listener, and my aim was always to lead by example.

Business analysis planning

Planning and scheduling are usually performed by a leader, or in some cases by a senior business analyst. It encompasses:

- determining and planning activities that business analysts will perform on a project
- agreeing what deliverables will need to be produced by the business analyst
- agreeing to how the business analysts will control and manage changes to the deliverables
- defining stakeholders required to be engaged (using what is known as a stakeholder matrix)
- defining the communication plan.

Planning and scheduling are clearly defined in the BABOK® Guide as a first task in the business analysis planning and monitoring phase.

There is often little time upfront to plan business analysis activities on projects. As a lead and senior business analyst working on several projects, I am expected to provide a plan for the business analysis activities. Depending on the project you are working on, different approaches can be used to estimate the appropriate timeframes needed to define requirements.

Agile estimates will differ from Waterfall estimates. Effort estimates will start out with a high degree of variability and be refined as a business analyst comes to clearly understand the project, assignment and timelines.

You may decide to estimate the requirements activities based on complexity. I've used the following estimation matrix on several projects, as a rough rule of thumb:

Simple = 1 to 2 weeks
Medium = 2 to 4 weeks
Complex = 4 to 6 weeks

These timeframes can be adjusted based on your experience and the needs of the project. You may find the estimates on Agile projects can be based on the points system. For example, the estimation poker method can be used for estimation purposes.

Key business analyst skills that play a big part in this competency are analytical thinking and problem-solving, with the ability to provide input and support decision-making and business cases.

As a lead business analyst, I've been involved in initial planning workshops and meetings, providing input to critical stakeholders, project managers and other team members involved in the initial discussions. Typically, during this planning phase, companies will start reviewing the proposed project, understanding key goals and values, and how these values are aligned to overall organisational goals. Additionally, high-level costing and benefits are also provided. This information will support decisions made from a priority perspective, and which project may or may not make it into a particular financial year's budget.

The business analyst (usually at senior, lead levels) will provide a supporting business analysis plan for each project or initiative with the information they have at hand.

KEY TAKEAWAYS

- Assess and undertake your skills audit on an ongoing basis.
- As a leader, make sure you have established an effective business analysis practice.
- Ensure you have the right balance of the BA competency levels in the BA practice or organisation by upskilling and encourage continuous learning.
- Conduct BA professional development (mentoring, coaching, training) for your team.

ACTION YOU CAN TAKE

You must allocate time to assess your own skills. I evaluate my skill set on based on my 90-day plans, set at the beginning of each year, in January. I set my career and personal goals, combined with individual tasks I want to achieve.

Activity 6.1. 90-day activity plan template

Use this 90-day activity plan to set yourself up for success.

Focus – I set my objectives for 30, 60 and 90 days.

For example: setting up a business analysis community of practice (BA COP).

Goals – I set goals that achieve my objectives.

For example: seek to understand if there is any other COP in the organisation. Identify who needs to be involved. Set up regular BA COP meetings.

Priorities – I outline high-level priorities that should be completed first in each month.

For example: Identify who needs to be involved in BA COP, by sending an email to potentially interested parties. Talk to senior executives in the company to see if they are aware of any COP. Gain an understanding if they would find value in BA COP.

Metrics of success – BA COP working group has been set up. BA COP meetings have been scheduled for every fortnight for one year.

30 days

Focus	Goals	Priorities	Metrics of success

60 days

Focus	Goals	Priorities	Metrics of success

90 days

Focus	Goals	Priorities	Metrics of success

Chapter 7

Skills required to be a good business analyst

Be your own leader in delivering requirements.

Be your own leader in delivering business analysis. We are all leaders in some way or another. I'm a leader of my team and a leader of my kids, especially my teenage daughter. You can be a leader in delivering business analysis outcomes on time and to a high standard by:

- Regularly undertaking a competency skills audit. It is essential to spend time running through your competency skills (which include core and complementary skills) and doing an audit. This is further described in the competency model. Think about what you are doing now and prepare to achieve more. What are your goals? What will you prioritise that can be done next?
- Ensure you have a clear understanding and practice these key techniques:
    - Brainstorming. Pull out and start using brainstorming maps. These are useful in assessing ideas and topics.
    - Ask 'Why?' often. It is an excellent business analysis approach. There is a lot of information available on the 'Why' theory should you wish to learn more (for example, *The 5 whys process we use to understand the root of any problem* by Courtney Seiter[14]).
    - Conducting interviews and workshops to understand the current state and gather ideas on the future state of your organisation or a project you are working on.

Skills required at different levels

It is also important to consider business analysts levels. Reflecting on the BA evolution described in the Evolution of business analysis section, the following is a summary of different levels of business analysts and the core knowledge areas required at each level.

14 C Seiter, 'The 5 Whys Process We Use to Understand the Root of Any Problem', buffer.com, buffer.com, 9 September 2018, accessed 14 February 2023.

Business analyst level	Proficiency	Knowledge area
Junior	General awareness	Elicitation and collaboration, requirements management
Business analyst	Practical knowledge	Elicitation and collaboration, requirements management, skills and techniques
Senior business analyst	Skilled	Business analysis planning and monitoring, elicitation and collaboration, requirements management, skills and techniques
Lead business analyst	Expert, strategist	Planning and monitoring, strategic analysis
Business analyst manager	Expert	Business analysis planning and monitoring, strategic analysis, people management

The competency level diagram on the following page is useful to assess priority. It was created by my friend, a Strategic Adviser with IIBA, Michael Augello, and it is used with permission here.[15]

Use this capability model quadrant as a sample to prioritise and assess your skills.

Once you assess yourself, I highly recommended that you create an action plan. The action plan should contain the goals you want to achieve, and by when. In my career, I've always tried to create my path by finding opportunities to grow myself. I recall the time Agile methodology was introduced to the IT industry and I wanted to gain some experience in this space. An opportunity presented itself and I put my hand up to be the first project to pilot Agile methodologies and the organisational transformation to the new ways of working. This experience personally uplifted me.

15 Sourced from IIBA Competency Assessment presentation (Unlock your BA and Leadership Potential) [unpublished training materials], by M Augello, 2022, accessed 13 February 2023.

Figure 7.1 Key competencies to consider when assessing your level

From a leadership perspective, it is important to inspire your team and encourage them to continue developing the most useful skill set. Understand your team's capabilities, rate them (check out the competency matrix I have included in the coming pages) and work on succession plans. You need to understand what type of work inspires them and help them work towards their goals. (This may not necessarily align to your individual goals from a leadership perspective, so it is a balancing act.)

I recommend using these best practice industry standards to assess whether your skills are at a recognised standard. Be honest with yourself; assess and determine your gaps. What are your gaps based on where you want to be?

To build strong skills and create a good team, you need to assess each competency and work on the action plans. Use the following competency rating matrix as a basis to assess yourself or your team members on a scale from 1 to 5. The competency matrix description is based on the business analysis competency model v4 by IIBA and has been constructed based on my experience.

Activity 7.1. Competency rating matrix

Rating	Label	Description
5	Expert	Challenges the status quo to develop innovative solutions that help advance business analysis as a discipline, practice or profession. Helps expand business analysis concepts and practices. *Usually in business analyst lead or enterprise or strategic analyst role.*
4	Advanced	An advanced business analyst will: – address any challenge or opportunity, regardless of the level of complexity – find a way to deliver business value for any change challenge – guide and mentor others to help them deliver better business outcomes – be sought after for expertise and guidance in addressing business challenges – provide insight into situations that fall within (or outside of) your sphere of influence. *Generally, senior business analysts are in these roles. In some instances, senior business analysts become product owners as well.*

Rating	Label	Description
3	Intermediate	An intermediate-level business analyst will: – successfully complete straightforward tasks and smaller, well-scoped challenges independently – identify appropriate actions and modifications. Guidelines have been provided to address a challenge. *Generally a middle-level business analyst that has had more than two years of BA experience.*
2	Foundational	The foundational level describes someone who: – needs and follows the rules and guidelines to perform tasks – adheres to prescribed ways of working to execute competency activities – recognises the key elements of the competency and why they are important. *Generally a business analyst with a few years of experience who is still learning in the role.*
1	Limited knowledge	The limited knowledge level describes someone who has a fundamental awareness and understanding of basic skills and knowledge involved in the competency. Generally, junior business analysts. Someone that has just started out in a BA career.

To further work on your skills audit assessment, use this capability assessment as a starting point.

Activity 7.2. Capability assessment template

Core competencies	Description	Your competency level Limited knowledge 1	Foundational 2	Intermediate 3	Advanced 4	Expert 5
Planning and monitoring	Organise and coordinate tasks, and work effort required to perform business analyst tasks.					
Strategic analysis	Perform work to collaborate with stakeholders to identify a need of strategic or tactical importance (the business need).					
Requirements elicitation	Conduct elicitation activities, obtain information from stakeholders and confirm results.					
Requirements management	Deliver requirements analysis, documentation, requirements life cycle management.					
Techniques	Provide a means to perform business analysis tasks with the most common techniques.					
Business knowledge	In-depth knowledge in key business areas, e.g., superannuation, insurance, products.					
Technical knowledge	In-depth technical knowledge in the current market, e.g., cloud, Assure, infrastructure.					

And for further elaboration into underlining competencies, use the following table. The purpose of each competency is to define an appropriate method to conduct business analysis activities.

Activity 7.3. Underlying core competencies assessment template

Underlying core competencies	Description	Limited knowledge 1	Foundational 2	Intermediate 3	Advanced 4	Expert 5
	Planning and monitoring					
Plan business analysis approach	**Brainstorming.** Identify possible business analysis activities, techniques, risks and other relevant items to help the business analysis approach. **Document analysis.** Review existing organisational assets that might assist in planning the approach. **Interviews** assist with building BA plan. **Lessons learned.** Identify any previous enterprise lessons learned. **Process modelling.** High-level processes define and document the business analysis approach. **Survey or questionnaire** are used to identify possible business analysis activities, techniques, risks and other relevant items to help build the business analysis approach. **Best practice tools,** methodologies and template processes.					

You can further elaborate on these based on the competency and techniques described in Part 2: Skills required to get business analysis right and build the best BA team.

Ownership and accountability are essential for any good business analyst, so always take ownership of the project and take pride in your work. Proactively drive key outcomes and be pleased at the end that you were able to deliver something successfully. That way, when you move on to your next project, you can talk enthusiastically about the real impact you had and not have to hide behind others' work.

Make sure you conduct practical requirements and business needs elicitation, running effective meetings to ensure needs are captured at the right time.

Add value by having a voice. While your role is centred around making things happen, you should also have the autonomy to have a voice and make suggestions on how processes could be improved or, in some cases, be wholly reinvented. That way, you will add value while also earning credibility. Respecting each other matters, as does being open and honest.

The standout for me is to facilitate effective meetings and workshops by ensuring:

- the right stakeholders are engaged and there is strong engagement with you
- there is trust; explain to your stakeholders clearly what is in it for them
- if you need to have difficult conversations, make sure you prepare.

How to use different methodology types

As business analysts, we get to know the environment and people; hence, we must be adaptable to working in different environments and producing quality requirements.

The following are typical requirements methodology types predominately used to manage projects and gather requirements.

- **Waterfall**

This traditional software development life cycle (SDLC) model encompasses sequential development through the typical project phases.

- **Agile**

This approach is well known for the team's short development cycles, co-location and collaboration.

- **Rapid application development (RAD)**

This approach encompasses building solutions in parallel with documentation and integrating all components at the end of the project.

- **Prototyping**

In this approach, the solution is built from the mock-ups or components of the system to support proof of concept.

Although Agile methodology seems to be commonly used in many organisations these days, I've discovered the Waterfall and hybrid approaches are still commonly used in many too. When working in different environments you need to be flexible in the approach you use with stakeholders. As a team, you will agree on which methodology bests suits your organisation or project.

It is important that the whole team is prepared to work in a certain way and attend the daily stand-up meetings, and that there is a commitment from the team to be transparent and work together.

Agile ways of working encourage continuous collaboration and sharing information. I have found this an effective way of working as it leads to avoiding misinterpretation. Some companies may choose a more hybrid approach, selecting parts of the Agile methodology that suit them. You will need knowledge and courage to be adaptable and work in these environments.

Requirements somewhat will need to be more than 50% right. In the Agile environment where the delivery of requirements is time-boxed, the requirements need to be validated and right for delivery. So, it is important to get them close to 100% right.

Other input that plays a big part in getting requirements right is having the right stakeholders with the right knowledge. For example, if the SMEs allocated to your project do not have extensive knowledge of the subject, or don't have a clear view on what they want the future to look like, it can be difficult to make sure requirements are right. You could end up with change requests being raised and an undesirable product delivered.

In an Agile environment, you will find additional changes to the user stories during showcase sessions, when users see the product. It is important that these changes are appropriately managed.

Try to get requirements right in a limited time; you must get the user stories completed in time. And I know it can be challenging, getting everything done on time. Make sure your requirements are done and right.

Whilst working on many Agile (and hybrid) projects, I have ensured that all my user stories were reviewed and validated and that some form of approval was provided by a stakeholder. I understand that in this environment the requirements need to be easy for delivery at a fast pace, hence the user stories need to be ready prior to an interaction (aka sprint). Depending on my stakeholder, I have made sure user stories for the next sprint are ready in advance. If my stakeholder was not comfortable with Jira, I would extract the EPICS and user stories from Jira and send them to my stakeholder in PDF or Word format. I would ask my stakeholder to review the EPICS and user stories and provide their feedback via email.

In the Waterfall approach, you will be tasked with delivering requirements documentation at specific phases of a project (not in small timebox intervals like in Agile projects). These documents, once approved, are shared with downstream teams such as design, development, implementation and testing.

Being a people leader and a recruiter, I've found that some individuals struggle when moving between and working with different methodologies. It seems more important when they move from working in an Agile environment to Waterfall approaches and having to deliver high-level quality business requirements documentation. When working in Agile environments and delivering user stories, there are different expectations and specific templates for the delivery of business requirements documentation.

I have seen individuals struggle to shift to writing BRD documentation (especially if they have only worked in Agile environments). The quality of the BRD can somewhat be diminished. So, make sure that you take extra care, spend your spare time in peer-to-peer reviews and create many individual draft versions that are reviewed before sending them to your key stakeholders and sponsors. If you don't have a generic BRD template, there is much research you could conduct on the internet, or reach out to me.

The SAD and prototyping approaches can be used on an as needs basis. I've worked using these methods in smaller, start-up companies. There are close interactions with the customers, and projects are of a smaller scale, for example, improving the configuration of their products. I have enjoyed working with them, building that initial relationship with the stakeholders, and taking them through an IT project journey, explaining the terminology.

And lastly, if you need confidence, or don't want to be asking your peers or managers for help, or are unsure how to work in different environments, undertake mentorship or coaching programs. I find mentorship or coaching programs tailored to your needs work the best. I have use cases on individually tailored mentorship programs for roles such as portfolio analysts and test managers, with a career path in business analysis. Carmen (not her real name) wanted to pursue a career in business analysis. I have created a tailored mentorship program for her with real life examples, relating to her current workplace. Carmen was quick to grasp and learn business analysis concepts, whilst measuring her knowledge gaps against the competency matrix described in this chapter. Carmen currently holds a business analyst role.

KEY TAKEWAYS

- The business analysis world is complex. Businesses achieve competitiveness by using technology to reach more customers. And the business analyst plays a crucial role in understanding and defining the technology needs and business vision, and making the business vision a reality.

- You *can* get the business analysis right. You may need to be creative, but it is possible. There is a plethora of information on this topic available.
- Actively listening to stakeholders and understanding their pain points is valuable.
- Assess and undertake your skills audit on an ongoing basis.
- As a leader, ensure you have the right balance of the BA competency levels in the BA practice or organisation by upskilling and encourage continuous learning.
- Conduct BA professional development (mentoring, coaching, training).

ACTION YOU CAN TAKE

- You must allocate time to assess your capability and rate yourself. Reflect on this chapter on to evaluate yourself and assess which level you might be.
- Use *Activity 7.1. Competency rating matrix*, *Activity 7.2. Capability assessment template*, and *Activity 7.3. Underlying core competency assessment template* to determine your level in the capability matrix. Follow this by setting yourself goals and tasks in the areas of what you desire to achieve, by using the *Activity 6.1. 90-day activity plan template* in Chapter 6.
- If you are a leader, you should set up 1:1 or group leader team meeting to assess individuals in your team. I have asked each of my team members to assess themselves first, using activities described in this chapter. I found holding my leadership team meeting every six months, working through the capability assessments prepared by individuals and then my leadership team providing their assessment thoughts an effective way of assessing my team's capability. We followed this by creating 90-day plans for individuals and teams.

Conclusion

7 key ingredients to get business analysis right

Successfully transition and work effectively in different environments.

It is really like art ... so many components to think about. Lots of different parts and skill sets to consider. The art of getting the business analysis right can be tricky.

A lot has been covered so far. Let's put it all together.

So, what does it take to do it well?

Just like an engine funnel, so here are the key seven business analysis ingredients required.

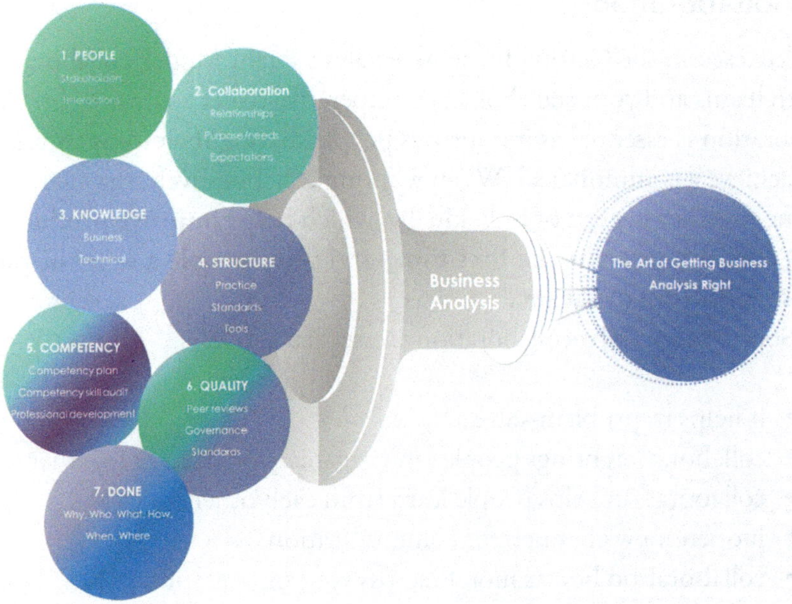

Figure 8.1. The seven ingredients funnel

1. People

It is all about working closely with people and stakeholders (including your team members), and your interactions with them. Here is how I've applied neuroscience and cognitive theory. When dealing with people, you must:

- stay connected with your stakeholder groups and ensure you are on the same page

- ask the RIGHT questions
- gain the CONFIDENCE and TRUST of the stakeholder
- share information and raise flags
- deal with conflicting points of view
- pick up on missed body language and other cues on how someone is feeling or behaving
- understand WHY things are done a certain way.

2. Collaboration

As covered in the Getting Business Analysis Right Model, collaborating with teams and your stakeholders is imperative to get analysis right. Collaboration is essential as it improves people sharing their ideas and skills to achieve a common goal. When working collaboratively, the analysis is done together instead of individually, which **helps improve productivity, gets things right the first time, and gives people a sense of purpose in the organisation**.

Some reasons why collaboration is essential are:

- it helps us problem-solve
- collaboration brings people (and organisations) closer together
- collaboration helps people learn from each other
- it opens new channels for communication
- collaboration boosts morale across your organisation
- it leads to higher retention rates.

Build solid relationships with the people you work with. Take them out for a coffee (virtual coffee if you are still not back in the office), lunch or even a drink – food and beverages build strong relationships.

The key tip or trick when facilitating conversations to understand client and stakeholder needs is to ask open-ended questions such as:

- What is the most important feature you might find helpful here?
- What is new that you would like to share or see?
- How would you like this feature to look?

What do you see your organisation looking like in five years?

Set the right expectations with your stakeholders and team members. Discuss your role and responsibility, your deliverables and what is expected of them as stakeholders, as well as your team members. You will find yourself working closely with change analysts and change managers, maybe even process analysts if you have them on your project. Change teams rely on detailed deliverables to do their job.

When everybody comes together and works as one, **workflows become smoother, activities can be achieved quickly and effectively, healthy, trustful relationships can be formed, and, as a result, the quality of analysis is improved**. Without a doubt, this, in turn, boosts morale, improves everyone's motivation levels and benefits everyone in the long run.

3. Knowledge

Business

As covered in previous sections of this document, having experience and an understanding of the processes, workflows and key aspects of the business, referred to as business domain knowledge, is important to business analysis.

Domain knowledge such as banking, superannuation, insurance, and manufacturing provides a competitive advantage as you can more easily and quickly identify the business needs and current state and provide value add by suggesting improvement areas.

Domain knowledge comes with experience and years of working in business analysis.

Technical

Business analysts should have some technical skills for precise and practical analysis, and it is essential to keep up-to-date with technical knowledge in this constantly changing environment. For example, SQL database, business intelligence, reporting, Azure and cloud environments.

Some projects that are more technical in nature (implementation of cloud solutions, etc.) will require a technical business analyst. Business analysts in these environments must know how to pull, analyse and report on data trends, document data or interface requirements, and share information with business stakeholders.

4. Structure

The proper structure includes the best industry-standard tools to support the delivery of analysis.

5. Competency

As outlined in the Getting Business Analysis Right Model section, competency includes having a competency plan, conducting a competency skills audit and continuous professional development to stay in the game with new technology trends and improvement methodologies.

For your team or you to continue to develop professionally or personally, you need to have a competency model and a plan to support the competency trajectory you have created for yourself.

The journey I undertook to create the competency model for my clients was to understand the roles they had interest in and then provide them with pathways they might take.

Business analysts are in demand. Clients have approached me to help them with their career path and help them understand what it means to be a business analyst, for example.

The first questions I asked them are:

- What do they like doing?
- What don't they enjoy doing?
- What are their immediate and long-term goals, and target five-year journey?

As the business analyst field is expanding in different industries and types of projects (Agile, Squad, traditional Waterfall), demand has driven individuals to consider becoming business analysts, for example SMEs.

Most companies have realised the need for business analytical skill sets and the value business analysis can provide. These skills are important to the organisation for management to make the right decisions.

Throughout my career, I've had an exciting journey that is still evolving. I'm now using my business analysis leadership skills in a Technology Engagement Manager role. My role incorporates analysis, project management and relationship building. Everything I've learned over my career informs my current work.

I have created a business analysis competency assessment, aligned to some areas identified in the IIBA BABOK® Guide, to assist with assessing your skill set and to provide you with a professional career path.

6. Quality

Quality controls need to be in place.

So, what does quality control mean in the context of business analysis. Well, in everything we do, quality control is an essential part.

Quality control (QC) ensures quality and procedures are adhered to. It sets out guidelines, such as standards and governance. Conducting peer reviews with your team members will assist with your journey to quality deliverables.

Have a high-quality, clear standard of what *good* looks like.

Write effective requirements and tailor project methodology and templates to meet:

- an organisation's context and complexity
- a project's size and complexity.[16]

7. Done

And finally, the definition of done. Having a purpose in getting business analysis DONE is as essential as any other ingredient. It is generally where there is an agreement with a team and a set of criteria that must be

16 M Montgomery, 'The art of tailoring to project methodologies and templates to deliver effective / concise requirements on your projectmedium.com', Analyst's corner medium.com, 17 May 2020, accessed 5 February 2023.

met to be recognised. From a business analysis perspective, I would like you to think about:

Why is analysis required?

- Who needs the analysis and have these stakeholders been engaged?
- What do they need the analysis for, and has the purpose been achieved?
- How is the analysis required to be completed, and have they been completed as required?
- When are the requirements needed to be completed, and have they been completed on time?
- Where is business analysis required? And has it been completed?

The main questions of *why, who, what, how, when and where* will prompt you to have all aspects of business analysis covered and get it right.

ACTION YOU CAN TAKE

Regardless of the level you are at as a business analyst, remember to use the seven ingredients to make sure you have clearly understood what will make you get business analysis right.

Activity 7.1. 7 ingredients for getting business analysis right checklist

Ingredients	Description	Yes/No
People	Are you connected with your key stakeholders by asking the right questions?	
	Do they understand why things are done a certain way?	
	Are you sharing information and raising any concerning flags?	
	Have you gained their confidence and trust?	
Collaboration	Have you set the right expectation with your stakeholder/s?	
	Have you discussed your role and responsibility with your stakeholder/s?	
	Have discussed with your stakeholder what is expected of your team, them and you?	
Knowledge	Do you have required business domain knowledge?	
	Do you have required technical domain knowledge?	
Structure	Do you have right industry best practice standards and tools to support the delivery of analysis?	
Competency	Do you have the right competency plans?	
	Have you conducted a competency skills audit of your team and yourself?	
	Have you created a professional development plan for you and your team?	
Quality	Have you got the right quality control and procedures for you and your team to adhere to?	
	Have you got the right governance in place, and conducted peer reviews with your team members?	

Ingredients	Description	Yes/No
Done	Do you understand why business analysis needs to be done?	
	Do you know who needs the analysis?	
	Do you have a list of key stakeholders?	
	Do you understand how business analysis will be done?	
	Has business analysis been completed as required?	
	Do you understand when business analysis needs to be completed?	
	Has the business analysis been done?	
	Do you understand where business analysis needs to be done?	
	Has the business analysis been done on time?	

Closing thoughts

Business analysis can be done right. I have seen it.

By taking you back in time, acknowledging the business analyst role evolution and constant project framework changes (Agile, Waterfall), I wanted to show you the complexity of business analysis and why it can be challenging to get it right and on time.

Sometimes it feels like you are not getting where you want to go on projects and are dealing with difficult people daily. You might think: *Not that person or stereotype again. Not that project again.*

You can get business analysis right at least 50% of the time by applying key ingredients – people, collaboration, knowledge, structure, quality and your definition of done – and the techniques covered in this book.

And don't forget ownership. Make sure you take ownership of the project you are working on, take pride in your work and make sure you add value.

Good business analysts dig into the context and understand *WHY* and *WHAT* isn't being said. This can make a big difference in the impact and the results.

Be humble, be open-minded, don't upset people and be on good terms with everyone.

Try it.

Acknowledgments

After publicly speaking on the art of getting business analysis right at many events, I have decided to write a book on this popular topic. I never thought I would be writing my first of what will hopefully be many books to come.

Special thanks to my family (my husband Rob Montgomery, my son Eavan DiRienzo and daughter Mia DiRienzo) for their ongoing support and understanding of all my special activities and passion projects, like writing this book. Their understanding is priceless; their tolerance of me with my laptop in hand doesn't go unnoticed.

Also, a special thank you to all the amazing business analysts, my mentees and my business analysis team at UniSuper for your support in creating a strong business analysis practice, whilst applying the principles and core skill sets described in this book.

Vicki Clarke – Solution Architect and a great friend. Thank you for your ongoing support, honest feedback and challenging and questioning the status quo to get this book in right. We spent long Sunday afternoons editing, restructuring this book and, of course, over a cheeky glass of rosé. Your friendship and support are invaluable.

Fabian Musci – Test Program Manager. Your support and honest feedback, from a testing perspective, are really appreciated. It is just what I needed to get it right.

Wendy Loo – Business Analyst Lead, now Iteration Manager. Your input into the process maps in this document and leading business analysis initiatives is beyond excellence. It was great having you and Kirsten Kiefer in my leadership team. We strive to establish the best business analysis practice, which led to being a finalist in the IIBA Business Analysis

Practice of the Year Awards in 2022. Such an excellent leadership and business analysis team effort.

Michael Augello – Strategic Advisor at IIBA and a great supporter of my passion for mentoring and coaching others. Your tremendous input and support in the capabilities uplift are greatly appreciated. It was great bouncing ideas, and sharing knowledge and stories from our experience and your great work. You inspire me!

Huge thank you to Louise Bedford – author, speaker, host of the trading podcast and co-owner of the trading game share trading company – and Maree Burgess – author, trainer, leadership coach and facilitator, for your ongoing encouragement and support to turn my passion, knowledge and speaking material into an eBook about getting business analysis right. Your friendship and catch-up dinners, at which I set my goal to get this eBook published and kept me accountable, have helped me enormously. Thanks, ladies, I am very lucky to have you by my side, providing ideas and being part of this journey with me. I appreciate you, our friendship and your support.

To my editor, Stephanie Preston: you are amazing. Thank you for you working with me, telling me what I was missing and enhancing this book to a high level of professionalism. You have certainly made this book look, feel and read to a high standard.

References and further reading

Arkhipov, 1 (2022), 'Quick Bite #5: BA health check questions', medium.com, accessed 15 February 2023.

Fishbeck, M, 'Customer Journey Mapping for Business Analysts', modernanalyst.com, accessed 10 February 2023.

Hass, KB (2011), 'The Enterprise Business Analyst: Developing Creative Solutions to Complex Business Problems', Berrett-Koehler Publishers.

Keller, H (2000), 'The Story of My Life', Dover Publications Inc.

IIBA (International Institute of Business Analysis), (2015), *A Guide to the Business Analysis Body of Knowledge* ***(BABOK® Guide)****, iiba. org,* accessed 13 February 2023.

Leffingwell, D (1999), 'Managing Software Requirements', Addison Wesley Publisher.

Malloud, OZ (2020), *How to solve 50% of your problem?*

Martin, J, 'The Right Business Analyst, the Right Project', modernanalyst.com, accessed 13 February 2023.

Medellin, A (2022), 'The Business Analysist Job Outlook in 2023', Dataquest, Dataquest.io, accessed 18 February 2023.

Montgomery, M (27 April 2020), '7 Tips On How To Capture Requirements Effectively', medium.com, accessed 15 February 2023.

Montgomery, M (17 May 2020), 'The art of tailoring to project methodologies and templates to deliver effective / concise requirements on your project', medium.com, accessed 5 February 2023.

Montgomery, M (13 September 2020), 'Why non-functional requirements could be magical on your project and should not be overlooked', medium.com, accessed 15 February 2023.

Priest, C (2017), 'Computers Are Useless; They Only Give You Answers', DataRobot blog, accessed 14 February 2023.

Seiter, C (2018), 'The 5 Whys Process We Use to Understand the Root of Any Problem', buffer.com, accessed 14 February 2023.

Sinha, P (2022), 'The Art of Writing Good Documentation', medium.com, accessed 15 February 2023.

Seuss, Dr (1978), *I can read with my eyes shut!*, Random House UK.

Covey, SR(2020), 'The 7 Habits of Highly Effective People', Simon & Schuster Australia Publisher.

Wiegers, K (2019), 'The Habits of Effective Business Analysts', medium.com, accessed 15 February 2023.

Wiegers, K (2020), Requirements Review Challenges, medium.com, accessed 13 February 2023.

Wiegers, K (2023), When Bad Requirements Happen To Good People, medium.com, accessed 13 February 2023.

About the author

Maria Montgomery
Business Information Technology BSc
Professional Accounting MA
CPC, MCC

Just a little bit about me

I have a Master's in Professional Accounting and a Bachelor of Business in Information Technology. This facilitated my entry into my first business analysis job, straight out of university, many moons ago.

A great interest in human behaviour, cognitive theory and our brain, along with my passion to help individuals and teams saw me recently become certified as a Master Certified Professional Coach (MCP with ICF) and Certified Professional Coach (CPC with ICF). Additionally, I hold various certifications in neuro-linguistic programming (NLP), cognitive behaviour therapy (CBT) and practitioner accreditation (also very helpful in dealing with teenagers), which have helped me to acquire a greater understanding of cognitive science and neuroscience.

After many years of industry experience, coupled with ongoing study, I'm now a leader, mentor, trainer and speaker who specialises in assisting individuals and organisations to gain and grow business analysis skills.

I facilitate organisations and individuals to build strong capabilities to enable remarkable performance at work. I provide effective programs for individuals and organisations who want to build strong business analysis capabilities in their teams or for themselves.

And most importantly, I'm enthusiastic about analysis. Analysis is key in all aspects of life. It certainly helped me understand what happens if you fail to do proper analysis when my husband and I decided to open a small business – a sushi restaurant. Yes, we were impetuous enough to believe that we could spend less than 5% of our time on a side business to earn a supplementary income, whilst still working full-time. Of course, being new to small business, and new to sushi, it consumed more than 10% of our personal time. However, my analytical mindset came in handy on many occasions. For example, I couldn't believe it when one of our staff members asked me to draw process maps instead of written procedures; they could relate better to a visual process. To reduce the demands on my time to find a quicker way to train staff and make them more efficient, I captured all the process maps in flow charts. The graphic form overcame language difficulties and was used by staff as required. I was so happy to be able to bring my skills to a completely new environment; it was amazing.

I'm a regular contributing author on medium.com and in publications such as *Analysis Corner* and the *IT Growth GUILD* and am a speaker on various topics in the IIBA (International Institute of Business Analysis) and PMI (Project Management Institute) communities.

With over a decade of experience in business analysis and leadership, I help people acquire the right set of skills, enjoy what they do and get their work done the right way. I'm a strong believer that quality work is possible whilst still enjoying what you do if you master the right set of skills for the work you are expected to do.

My journey to Australia

My family and I arrived in Australia in 1986, my parents purchased a one-way ticket and Australia was to be our new home. We left behind immediate family, our house and the whole life we once lived. My mum and dad told me that we would be back in Kragujevac (the second biggest town in Serbia) in three months if we didn't like it here. Thirty-four years later, we have firmly established our lives in Melbourne. Straight after we landed at Melbourne Airport, we headed to the migration centre (at the time there was a centre set up for migrants coming to Melbourne to help our initial set up in Australia), where we stayed for around a month.

This was the first time I was exposed to different cultural backgrounds. It was a shock to the system. My parents had lots of problems to solve. Where to live, where to send me to school, how to find full-time jobs to support us. Happily, one thing they did work out quickly was where we could get fresh food – Footscray Market. Eating bananas in Serbia at the time was a luxury (we couldn't afford them). I remember eating so many of them when we arrived, and they tasted so good. Another great luxury was finding M&M's. They were so tasty, nothing like what we had in Serbia.

I have a childhood memory of Serbia: my father struggling to make ends meet and driving a small car that was a Fiat 770 running. With the amount of rust on the bottom of the car, he had to put a board on the bottom of it to drive us around. The board was a temporary solution to his problem. Even with his struggles, I recall him waking up every morning happy and going to work. He wanted more for his life and family. So, he searched for a better life somewhere else, in another country, a country where the whole family could escape.

I started my career in the airline industry in a company called Ansett (it no longer exists). I had business analyst opportunities and developed these skills to create a career path that traversed the logistics, financial, superannuation and health sector industries.

My analytical path and mindset

Along my journey of working for many different companies, I became a jack of all trades; stepping into different roles as expected by the companies I was working for. I learned the hard way how to get **high-quality** work done **on time**.

Now in a leadership role, managing people and relationships, setting up business analysis practices, mentoring, coaching, training, and yes, my list goes on. I like to be busy.

I also remind myself that I have been in business analysis for a long time (ouch!) and may have been born with a naturally gifted analytical mindset. I remember during my childhood, I drove my family up the wall, always asking questions, overanalysing everything. They probably thought I was whacky. But I love analysis, and I hope you do too.

MariaMontgomery.net
Instagram: @mariamontgomery3010
https://www.facebook.com/mmariamontgomery
Twitter: @MMongomery

Team up with me

I trust that you have enjoyed reading *The art of getting analysis right* and learning from my experience.

My belief is that everyone has the ability to learn a new skill that can dramatically improve your or your team's performance. I also believe that one of the best ways to learn something is to learn from others and their experience, and practise, keep on practising.

My vision is to compel individuals, leaders and organisations through coaching, training, and professional and personal development.

"According to the U.S. Bureau of Labour Statistics (BLS), the country's most authoritative source for career outlook, business analysts are on track for growth of up to 25% by 2030. It's a far cry from the country's 8% average growth expected by 2030."[17]

Business analysis skills are valuable for everyone and should be part of our lives. Every organisation's project needs to complete an effective business analysis to answer a critical question: "What are your key requirements?" It is all about understanding your *why*, then your *what*, to know your outcome and business value.

I help organisations and individuals build their business analysis capability and the right set of skills. As a passionate leader and coach, an expert in business analysis, I continue to publish articles and provide training and coaching.

It is your responsibility as an individual to:

17 A Medellin, 'The Business Analysist Job Outlook in 2023', Dataquest, Dataquest.io, 21 June 2022, accessed 18 February 2023.

- develop right skills to get business analysis right, and become a good business analyst
- find your career development gaps, personally and professionally and develop yourself.

As a leader, you must:

- lead the team in getting business analysis right
- develop the best business analysis team an organisation can have
- guide and support your team members to reach their full potential.

It would be great to hear how you are going with your business analysis, or your personal or professional development. Send me an email to mariamontgomery30@gmail.com.

Reach out to me via MariaMontgomery.net to book me for:

- leadership or individual coaching programs that will expedite your career growth
- a training program to learn and uplift your analysis skills to the next level.

It will be fantastic to work with you.

Made in the USA
Monee, IL
03 November 2026

67384044R00079